This Will Hurt

The Restoration of Virtue and Civic Order

edited by
Digby Anderson

Published by
The Social Affairs Unit

A National Review Book

*With thanks to the William H. Donner Foundation
for its contribution to the costs of the research
which made this book possible*

British Library Cataloguing in Publication Data
A catalogue record for this book is available from the British Library

Library of Congress Catalog Card Number: 95-069415

ISBN 0-907631-63-0

Printed in the United States of America

Contents

The Authors

Dr. Michael D. Aeschliman taught English at Columbia and the University of Virginia for 10 years and is now Director of the Erasmus Institute, Lausanne, Switzerland. He is author of *The Restitution of Man: C. S. Lewis and the Case Against Scientism* and edited a new paperback edition of Malcolm Muggeridge's 1934 novel *Winter in Moscow*. He has written widely for journals on both sides of the Atlantic. His selection of essays by John Henry Newman will be published shortly.

Professor William B. Allen is Dean and Professor, James Madison College, Michigan State University. His interests include political philosophy, American government, jurisprudence, and political economy. He taught formerly at Harvey Mudd College in Claremont, California. He has been a Kellogg National Fellow, Fullbright Fellow, member of the National Council on the Humanities, and member and Chairman of the U.S. Commission on Civil Rights. He is author of *Let the Advice be Good: A Defense of Madison's Democratic Nationalism* and editor of several collections, including *George Washington: A Collection* and *The Essential Antifederalist.*

Dr. Digby Anderson is founder Director of the Social Affairs Unit and editor of the Unit's series, *The Moral Dimension of Social Policy*. He was contributing editor of *The Loss of Virtue: Moral Confusion and Social Disorder in Britain and America*, published as a National Review Book. He is a regular contributor to journals and newspapers.

Professor F. H. Buckley teaches corporate and bankruptcy law at George Mason University School of Law in Arlington, Virginia, and has written extensively in those areas.

Dr. Christopher Dandeker is Senior Lecturer in the Department of War Studies, King's College, London, where he teaches civil-military relations and military sociology. His publications include *Surveillance Power and Modernity* and a recent article, 'New Times of the Military: the Changing Role and Structure of the Armed Forces of the Advanced Societies'.

Professor Christie Davies is Professor of Sociology at the University of Reading, England. He has been visiting lecturer in India, the United States, and Poland. He is the author of *Permissive Britain* and co-author of *Wrongful Imprisonment* and of *Censorship and Obscenity*. He has also published many articles on morality in scholarly journals on both sides of the Atlantic.

Professor Douglas J. Den Uyl is Professor of Philosophy and Director of the Master of Arts in Liberal Studies Program at Bellarmine College. He has written books and articles in the areas of social and political theory and ethics.

Rabbi Daniel Lapin is President of Toward Tradition and founding rabbi of Pacific Jewish Center, Venice, California. He started Toward Tradition in 1991 as a coalition of Christians and Jews, who felt more united by a common Judeo-Christian ethic than they felt separated by differing theologies. One of his goals is to educate business professionals about the moral and philosophical infrastructure that empowers ethical capitalism.

Professor Ross Lence is Associate Professor of Political Science at the University of Houston, Texas. He is a prolific contributor to scholarly journals on American political thought and author of *Union and Liberty: the Political Philosophy of John C. Calhoun*.

Professor Kenneth Minogue is a Professor of Political Science at the London School of Economics. His publications include *The Liberal Mind, Nationalism, The Concept of a University,* and *Alien Powers: The Pure Theory of Ideology*. He has also contributed widely to academic and intellectual journals and hosted a television series on free market economics, *The New Enlightenment*.

Professor Graeme Newman is Professor of Criminal Justice at the University of Albany. He has published many books and articles in the fields of punishment and comparative criminology. These include *Discovering Criminology, Vengeance: The Fight Against Injustice, The Punishment Response, Just and Painful Punishment,* and *Comparative Criminology*. His most recent work has focused on the role of communications media in shaping the public discourse on criminal justice. Professor Newman created the United Nations Crime and Justice Information Network in 1990, and has overseen its development since that time.

Professor Joseph F. Rychlak is the Maude C. Clarke Professor of Humanistic Psychology at Loyola University of Chicago. He has framed and empirically tested a teleological theory of human learning. His publications include *The Psychology of Rigorous Humanism, Artificial Intelligence and Human Reason: A Teleological Critique,* and *Logical Learning Theory: A Human Teleology and its Empirical Support.*

Linda Woodhead is Lecturer in Christian Studies at Lancaster University. She is the author of a number of articles on Christian ethics and on Christianity in the contemporary West. She is Editor of the journal *Studies in Christian Ethics.* Forthcoming publications include *An Introduction to Christianity* for Cambridge University Press.

Preface

Gertrude Himmelfarb

T
he most hopeful thing one can say about our present condition is that we have passed through the stage of denial and are prepared to confront our social problems. There are still die-hards, in the academy and the media, who protest that crime, illegitimacy, welfare dependency, and the like are exaggerated by fallacious statistics and a sensationalist press, or that they reflect a class and racial bias, or that they are the unfortunate consequences of the global economy. (In this post-cold war era, 'globalization' has replaced 'capitalism' as the epithet of choice.) But for most people, reality has asserted itself. We now know that what we have been experiencing cannot be denied, belittled, or explained away as anything but the moral crisis that it is.

But if we are no longer in a condition of cognitive dissonance, we are in a condition of confusion and indecision. What do we do about those problems that are undeniably with us? Here too most of us have advanced beyond the solutions of yesteryear. We no longer look to the state for salvation. The state—and more specifically, the welfare state—is now seen as part of the problem rather than the solution. Instead, we are beginning to think in terms of 'civil society', the institutions that mediate between the individual and the state: family, community, churches, local authorities, private enterprises, voluntary associations. (In the United States, the idea of trans-

Gertrude Himmelfarb, a historian who taught for twenty-three years at Brooklyn College and the Graduate School of the City University of New York, is the author of many books, including studies of Charles Darwin and Lord Acton. Her latest book, The De-moralization of Society: From Victorian Virtues to Modern Values, *was published by Knopf in 1995.*

ferring power from the national government to state governments, munici-palities, and civil society goes under the name of 'devolution'.)

This is a momentous change in our thinking and it is all to the good. But it is not sufficient. For civil society has been infected by the same virus that has contaminated the entire culture: irresponsibility, incivility, a lack of self-discipline and self-control. Indeed, the family itself, the keystone of civil society, is in disarray. Witness the prevalence of divorce, single-parent fam-ilies, fatherless children, illegitimacy, and promiscuity (particularly among teenagers).

It is evident that we are suffering from a grievous moral disorder. 'Social pathology' is the familiar term for the syndrome of crime, violence, promis-cuity, illegitimacy, drug addiction, and welfare dependency; 'moral pathol-ogy' would be more accurate. And that moral pathology requires strenuous moral purgatives and restoratives.

An earlier volume in this series is entitled *The Loss of Virtue*. The present volume examines the calculus of pains and pleasures required to restore virtue. The title, *This Will Hurt*, suggests that the pains may outweigh the pleasures. For a society that has prided itself on its tolerance and generosi-ty, that has denied and denigrated the sanctions that all previous societies have used to maintain virtue, to invoke those sanctions now is all the more difficult. One can almost say (as parents used to say to their children) that it hurts us more than them—society more than the delinquents and deviants in society. As respectable society has become more tender and forgiving, so the unrespectable (if one may use the old-fashioned language of virtue) have become more impervious to shame and guilt—'affectless', as the psycholo-gist puts it, 'conscienceless', the moralist would say.

It used to be the guiding principle of society (of all societies, but of liber-al societies preeminently) that social and moral sanctions are preferable to legal and penal ones, not only because the former are less harsh but also because they are more readily internalized in the individual. 'Society cannot exist', Edmund Burke reminds us, 'unless a controlling power upon will and appetite be placed somewhere, and the less of it there is within, the more there must be without'. For most of human history it was assumed that that power within—conscience, convention, religion, the moral sense—was a more humane mode of control than the coercive powers of the state.

The current fashion has it otherwise. It was part of Nietzsche's indictment of Christianity that the 'interiorization' of guilt in the form of sin and 'bad conscience' was far more cruel than any punishment a tyrant might inflict; self-punishment was the ultimate, the most devastating of punishments. This idea, popularized by Michel Foucault, has been the reigning doctrine in the universities for some time and is now appearing, in a watered-down version, in the popular culture. If anything is internalized, we are now told, it should be not conscience but self-esteem. 'Forgive yourself' is the mantra of psychotherapy. 'Blame someone else'—abusive parents or an oppressive society—is a standard defense in murder trials.

To reverse all of this, to undo the 'transvaluation of values' that Nietzsche has bequeathed to us, will be a painful process. It is easier and quicker to go downhill than uphill, to become de-moralized than to be re-moralized. Yet that process of re-moralization has to begin somewhere, and soon. *This Will Hurt* tells us just how painful—but also how rewardingthat re-moralization will be.

Introduction and Summary:

Rediscovering the Sources of Social Order

Digby Anderson

Rediscovering virtue

As the second millennium draws to a close the full extent of Western society's moral and social crisis is more and more apparent. America and Britain are indeed lands of plenty, rich countries, technologically sophisticated countries, whose citizens live long and healthy lives. But they are also lands of other and darker plenties, plenty of crime, plenty of gratuitous violence, plenty of children without fathers, plenty of fear, more and more alienation from public institutions such as government and law.

Increasingly, commentators are understanding that these problems will not be fixed by more welfare, higher expenditure on schools, more laws, more promiscuous rights. It is not newer, bigger, and better systems that are needed but better people. In the late 1990s there is at last a gradual understanding of what T. S. Eliot warned of in 1934, 'dreaming of systems so perfect that no one will need to be good'. So during these years there has been a renewed interest in the role of the virtues in understanding and combatting social problems and restoring social order. Words that some had thought and others hoped to see the back of forever are creeping back into social analysis: fidelity, duty, fortitude, toleration, honesty, self-reliance, manliness. And even those who are not ready to stomach the full range of the moral vocabulary are alluding to it collectively and indirectly when they talk of the need to promote 'community'.

But also waiting to be rediscovered, the ways societies attach people to good behaviour

But those who have rediscovered virtue or community rarely go on to the next and necessary part of the analysis which is to rediscover too the dynamics of virtue, the processes by which past societies *made* and kept people good. This also has a vocabulary waiting to be re-learned, re-understood, and turned into practice again. Older societies were not afraid to discuss and use conscience, guilt, pain, shame, ostracism, degradation, ridicule, stigma, authority, example, approbation, and uniformity to make men good and hold society together. Nor would they have been naive enough to imagine that a society could be maintained by using only the pleasant incentives, the carrots of example and approbation. They knew that men have bad, selfish, and destructive appetites which must be restrained and that civilization is a precarious thing. Protecting civilization and making men act against their evil appetites demands a large and varied armoury. Some of the best weapons in it are sharp and painful. Yet today's advocates of virtue and community shrink from admitting such truths. They prefer to dwell on the delights of community rather than honestly and realistically embrace the weapons necessary to achieve and sustain it. The politicians of yesteryear promised all sorts of policies and programmes without revealing the true cost in tax dollars and pounds. The politicians of today promise a revived community without mentioning the costs in terms of the pain and shame it will involve. The authors of this book are more honest. They know that the restoration of civic order will hurt. And they explain how.

The necessity of pain, shame, and stigma

It will hurt because, of their essence, that is what pain, shame, and stigma *do*. It will hurt much more because for every pain or shame actually inflicted, a hundred other persons will go in fear of pain and shame. That is how traditional moral systems work. They are societies of trepidation, circumspection, and anxiety. They are quite the opposite of today's self-affirmation, choose-your-own-lifestyle, whatever-you-are-happy-with climate. They value inhibition, self-control, and what the psychologists call repression, as necessary to civilized conduct.

Moreover, most of the armoury which can make men good is not in the hands of the police or the courts but takes place informally in the family, the street, the company or, in the case of conscience, inside people's heads. This is what makes it so powerful. To return America to law abidingness requires not a few more thousand policemen on the streets but over two hundred million policemen, each called conscience, all on twenty-four-hour duty, in each American's head. To restore family integrity requires not slightly tougher Social Security sanctions but a renewed sense of shame, of the devastation that once went with loss of respectability.

Conscience, shame, and respectability work. But it is obvious that they are not bureaucratic procedures. They are not explicit procedures. They are not centralised procedures. They are not, then, formally accountable procedures. The society that relies on conscience and shame lets loose forces that can go wrong, be misdirected or excessive. It should be concerned to minimise such wrongs, but it should be honest about their possibility. In yet another and related sense, 'this will hurt'. The workings of shame take place informally and even hypocritically. They employ what looks to the progressive mind like double standards. Like cases do not necessarily get treated alike. Individuals are 'made examples of'. The price of a society ordered by shame is that we abandon our high allegiance to openness. Let there be no misunderstanding: if the project to restore moral sensitivity is meant seriously, there can be no question but that this will hurt. Indeed, one test of whether morality is being seriously included in public policy on crime or illegitimacy will be precisely the volume and degree of outrage and anxiety produced.

Yet many of the contributors to this book think the venture worth the pain. As some suggest, there is no other way. Rabbi Daniel Lapin goes as far as to advocate measures that would stigmatise illegitimate children themselves, not just their mothers. When the stigma was stronger, he points out, fewer children were illegitimate and suffered it. Professor Graeme Newman suggests those seeking proper punishments for crime cannot deny themselves that huge range of painful and humiliating punishments used by previous societies. Professor Kenneth Minogue concludes that 'the authoritative order had first to be established by power and violence before it could solidify into the custom of authority', and that in the end its decline may only be halted by the recurrence of those conditions. Professor Michael Aeschliman finds progressive thinkers belatedly discovering the collapse of social order and eager to re-invent community. Yet this is to be done without any diminution of the various 'rights', especially that of personal autonomy and the individual's own self-chosen goals which produced the social disorder and which will make impossible any reinvention of community.

The price of restored community: reduced autonomy, the abandonment of egalitarianism, and a recognition of the limits of market forces

The path to virtue and social order through the disciplines of shame and stigma will hurt, then, in another sense: that it demands the giving up of various treasured modern ideas and practices. Personal autonomy is one. Another is egalitarianism: the social sanctions work by pointing out difference in worth, lauding the good, and inflicting pain or dishonour on the bad. With egalitarianism must go cultural relativism; the refusal to make judgements of worth as between cultures; and a certain view of science. It is, write Professors Aeschliman and Joseph Rychlak independently, that view of science which would reduce human action to what science can measure, and in so doing remove free will and personal responsibility.

If socialists must pay with their egalitarianism, those on the right must pay by recognising limits in the applicability of the market. Dr. Christopher Dandeker argues that it is trust and honour which hold together traditional institutions such as the military and the monarchy and that a narrow 'occupationalism' which treats them like companies risks destroying them.

Some of the processes by which men are attached to virtuous behaviour are at first sight less demanding. Yet approbation, at first sight a 'positive' incentive, acts by singling out the successful. It is what teachers in British schools reject under the epithet 'divisive'. It offends against egalitarianism. Uniforms offend for the same reason. The superficial identity they produce is a background against which genuine differences in ability and effort stand out even more starkly. Even love, the Christian dynamic of community, is no sentimental thing but a thoroughgoing way of life demanding a suffering and painful attachment to that which is good.

There are, of course, many sanctions, ways of making people good, which are not discussed here. Nor do the authors necessarily agree on what makes people good. What they do agree on is the importance of trying to regain an insight into the processes which integrate and disintegrate societies, which protect and undermine civilization, and that putting such a moral understanding of behaviour back into practice in public policy and community action will, in one way or another, hurt.

Guilt, shame, and embarrassment

The revolt against so-called Victorian values did not start in the 1960s as often supposed. It was well underway in the 1920s in, for example, Bloomsbury, and in versions of Freud which preached free expression, etc.

Even these had their roots in the 19th century, especially in its belief in progress and reason. But during the nineteenth century, one voice, points out Professor Aeschliman, in particular warned of the social consequences of over reliance on progress and reason. The prophet who foresaw the coming moral and social disintegration more surely than any other was Dostoevsky.

The revolt against the moral society was conducted under the banner of personal expression and its chief enemies were shame, guilt, and embarrassment—their equivalent in manners. But the new code of reason and self-indulgence is now confronted with crime, family collapse, and social disorder and is silent before them. It has belatedly taken to talking of the need for community but will not accept or admit the restrictions on personal expression that community demands. Dostoevsky understood the problem at the heart of Western society in a deep sense. He himself experienced the sense of rootlessness and absurdity which characterises it, though unlike other absurdists with whom he has been misclassified, Dostoevsky always hated it and knew its destructive power. His understanding was deep too, in that he does not just assert the dangers of a society morally adrift, unanchored by shame, but depicts it, shows it to his readers in minute detail, in the suffering souls of his characters and through his scenes of social life without embarrassment. The dangers are not theoretical. Societies can lose a sense of shame. Humaneness is only a habit. It can disappear from individuals and societies or be vanquished by other forces. And that is what is happening in the cities of the U.S. and Britain today.

In the end, Dostoevsky knew, it is not liberty or reason which will ensure sanity and order, but goodness, and the way to goodness lies through the disciplines of shame, guilt, and embarrassment.

When the law and shame conflict

Modern societies are increasingly unsuccessful at combining law and shame harmoniously and productively. Not only is there a tendency to ask too much of law, to seek a legal remedy when an informal social remedy will work better, but law, especially in the United States, is even undermining the operation of shame. Law, argues Professor Frank Buckley, is, in several ways, now detaching individuals from virtuous behaviour. The values of many modern laws are at odds with those traditional in American—and he might add British—families. This both subverts the traditional values and, by separating the ideas of damage and illegality from shame, threatens shame itself, one of the main ways in which societies attach people to virtuous behaviour.

Laws now can even make private virtuous behaviour illegal, as when landlords are punished for discriminating against unmarried couples who would be tenants. Some laws have always been at odds with 'common sense and morality' but the rule was that the two worked together. The most obvious instances of the widening gulf between law and popular morality are in criminal law, with the lightening of sentencing, the extension of parole, and the lowering of conviction probabilities. Here law damages social norms by doing too little. In other fields, such as tort law, it damages morality by doing too much. Actions now the province of law were once policed by social sanctions and such sanctions have been weakened by law's imperialistic intrusion. Moreover, by awarding damages for acts that commonsense morality does not think wrong, law has separated illegality from shame.

Excessive legal remedies, for instance, allowing claims for 'emotional distress', also damage virtue. They teach lessons against fortitude and circumspection. The expansion of law—and the damage done by it—may be explained as acts of money seeking or power seeking by lawyers. But they may also be explained as lawyers absorbing the degraded social norms of the time. There is thus a vicious circle in which law subverts popular morality and then is itself subverted by the new debased morality.

Ridicule as a way of protecting society from outlandish and socially costly ideas and practices

Ridicule may not have the high moral tone of shame. But it is, in fact, one of the chief defensive weapons of an orderly society secure in its values and assumptions, argues Dr. Digby Anderson.

If a robust and sophisticated sense of the ridiculous were here today, the acceptance and endorsement of deviant sub-cultures and the idiocies of political correctness would not last a moment. A number of Britain's and America's social ills, the growth of one-parent families, crime, AIDS, have not entered society on their own but have been accompanied by ideas and ideologies justifying, excusing, or asking for tolerance of the lifestyles that give rise to them. In this sense we may speak of dangerous ideas. The ideas were also, at the time of their introduction, outlandish. The idea that voluntary single parenthood was as valid as married family life was laughable. The idea that male sodomy was as normal as heterosexual intercourse was once dismissed outright. Indeed homosexual practice was regarded and listed as a perversion.

There is, then, a process by which ideas once outlandish and the behaviours they justify become accepted. The ideas and behaviours—and the social problems associated with them—spread and become mainstream. That process depends on the idea of debate, the modern notion that all ideas, however outlandish, have a right to be debated and that the debate should be conducted on grounds of the consequences of the behaviour associated with them. For instance, should a really outlandish idea and behaviour such as necrophilia be proposed for toleration it would typically be debated along the lines of who was hurt by the practice, were innocent others damaged, were there dangers to public health, or the unwisdom of using law to hound private behaviour. In short, the willingness to debate everything and the consequentialist and utilitarian rules by which such debates are conducted could find little reason for not permitting something as outlandish as necrophilia.

Older societies would not have let necrophilia get as far as debate. They would have ridiculed it, dismissed it out of hand. This capacity to ridicule and dismiss protected them better than rational debate protects modern society. These older societies had a more complex topography in which some ideas remained in the shadows, others were tolerated in the mainstream, and yet others were protected as public doctrine. They also had a respect for traditional learning and a readiness to practise its short-cut application in what are now denigrated as prejudices. If modern society is to be protected from outlandish ideas and behaviour, and all the problems they bring, it must recover its confidence to rule ideas out of court, its acceptance of the necessity of prejudice, and its sense of proportion and the humour which depends on it: the sense of the ridiculous.

The return to painful, public punishment

If modern societies are unwilling to use the informal sanctions, such as ridicule, which served former societies so well, they are similarly unwilling to use the more formal punishments associated with those societies. There is an absolute confusion among contemporary penologists about what to do with criminals. This is not because they have lots of competing suggestions. Quite the reverse. No new suggestions have emerged since the extended use of prison in the 19th century. Indeed, today's penologists effectively rule out the wide range of punishments their forebears could choose from, punishments which inflicted physical pain, punishments which removed the criminal from the community geographically (banishment) or socially (ostracism), punishments which left a stigma or mark (branding), punishments which mobilised public scorn (pillory, stocks, the dunce's cap in the corner), and especially punishments in public: what separates many of these from today's punishment is that these were morally based while today the justifications for punishment are political. Even 'treatment', now largely abandoned, was a moral justification.

Why has punishment been demoralised? asks Professor Newman. Because of two forces: first, the intrusion of science into social questions—social science—which has driven out value in the pursuit of an amoral 'objectivity'. Science replaces value with probability. It, unlike faith, is built on uncertainty. In the end, without value and morality, penology reaches a stage where it can see nothing to distinguish the criminal from the law abiding; nothing in his character, except his having been convicted as criminal. The other force is socialism, or rather socialism re-applied from classes to other groups and individuals. This too collapses distinctions between, say, criminals and law abiders in the name of equality. The murderer is no different from you and me except in his circumstances.

But, just as morality needs punishment, so punishment needs morality. A moral punishment, unlike a utilitarian punishment, involves criminal and punisher and society taking responsibility respectively for the criminal act and the punishment. This sort of punishment is the very opposite of prison, which hides punishment away. It is public at least in the sense that it is seen to be done, publicly willed, and taken responsibility for. It involves all parties recognizing the crime and punishment for what they are.

Uniforms and the maintenance of authority

Professor Douglas Den Uyl examines another way in which publicness maintains social authority—and which is also opposed by egalitarians. Two neglected requirements of the good society are that adults exert proper authority over children and that children be inhibited so as to acquire right desires. Uniforms in schools can both help these in practice and illustrate their importance in argument. Dress codes—restrictions on hair length, disapproval of jeans, etc.—and full-blown school uniforms are things of the past in American public schools. But they might have a part to play in any return to social order. Uniforms are worn by children but decreed by adults. They show that school is a process which children attend in order to become, eventually, part of the adult world. School uniform standards are not set by children. They further distinguish children from adults and proclaim that, at school at least, what adults offer is not companionship but authority and leadership.

Adults themselves accept dress codes, most obviously at work. Here they are a statement of serious intent. So in school the uniform indicates that this is a place of work not play. Uniforms, then, are beneficial in spelling out a relationship between adults and children that accords with the responsibilities implied by that relationship.

So why are they opposed? Uniforms superficially make all students look alike but, in fact, they upset radical egalitarians because, against this common background, differences in substantive achievements such as scholarship stand out more starkly. Moreover, they deny poor students a way of attaining peer esteem, by dress. The imposition of uniforms also offends progressives and multi-culturalists because it offends the formers' repudiation of inhibition and the latters' affirmation of diversity for its own sake. Students do not like wearing uniforms. Uniforms inhibit or repress their desires. But the desires they repress are juvenile not adult and trivial not substantive. Uniforms teach that self-expression and difference should relate to genuine achievement rather than trivia and educate desires into a civilized adult world.

The restoration of authority

Professor Kenneth Minogue analyses the more general passing of authority and what was lost with it. Authority was left for dead after the 1960s. The objection to it was not only that it was seen, wrongly, as the opposite of liberty, but that it could not provide instant and complete reasons for its practices.

Some authority, that of academic authorities, did have the reason of expertise, though even that had been acquired through respect for established knowledge. But much of the authority of the authority-figures so pervasive in the old society, from policemen to club officials, firemen to fathers, was a practical authority, useful because someone had to guide, because direction is better than confusion. Though it could be abused, this authority was often gentle. Much of it did not have the force of command and it was not intrusive into the self, merely asking for 'outward' compliance. It was accompanied by a distance and formality in social relations which left individuals a private world of freedom. It asked for formal compliance rather than enthusiasm.

What replaces authority may be more coercive, as was the case with Communism. It may be more manipulative, as is the case when negotiation succeeds authority and individuals intrude heavily into other selves in their attempt to cajole them to do what they wish—a growing feature of modern family life. Or it may involve harsher and more detailed rules: 'more and more areas of life subject to rules and, when contested, brought before courts and tribunals whose decisions, in spite of the elaborate codes by which they are governed, are increasingly arbitrary'.

These codifications and regulations destroy the spontaneous moral impulses which might begin to improve our situation. The end of the decline of authoritative order may only be halted by the things which established it in the first place, only after which it solidified into the softer custom of authority, namely power and violence.

Ostracism and stigma

Rabbi Lapin inspects the painful process for building authority and civilized order. Faced with soaring illegitimacy rates, rising violent crime, obscenity, and public disorder, both social scientists and lay people ask what the cause is. It is the wrong question. These things, a state of disorganization and degradation, entropy, are *natural.* Ask instead what miracle it was that once kept society safe, prosperous, well-mannered, and stable. For this is not a natural state at all. And since it is not a natural state, ask what special intelligence or energy initiated and maintained it. What did we *do* to produce such a state out of chaos?

The stable, safe, and courteous society had a whole armoury for maintaining itself, for fighting entropy. As the word suggests they were weapons. They hurt. Order depended on being willing to inflict pain. And not only physical pain but shame, disgrace, ostracism, and stigma. It was prepared too to inflict them on children, for example on illegitimate children.

There was a justification for this readiness to hurt in the cause of order. In the case of children, 'civilization depends upon maintaining a "community of the generations". Everything we do affects the generations to come, and either honours or dishonours our ancestors. . . . We know that our positive achievements and our monetary success benefit our children. Why should we expect that our sins will not harm them?' Moreover, the stigma is a deterrent weapon. When the stigma of illegitimacy was stronger, fewer suffered it for there were fewer illegitimate births.

Ostracism need not always be harsh. Social sanctions can be applied in varying degrees of intensity. Banishment is ostracism. So is the exclusion of a sloppy dresser from a prestigious business luncheon. The allocation of offices, desks, perks, and promotions, who is consulted about what, are testimony to the fine workings of sanctions in the corporation.

Moreover, even liberals, those who denounce ostracism and censure, use them. What else is Political Correctness or the coercive orthodoxy of the AIDS red ribbon or the hounding of smokers but the operation of good old-fashioned social sanctions, albeit in the service of new ideologies?

The distinction then is not between those who use and those who do not use such sanctions. All societies and stable orders need them. The distinction is between whether they are used in the service of God-given morality and the dignity of man, or in the service of God-denying materialism.

Respectability and approbation

If the ostracism and stigma called for by Rabbi Lapin will shock the progressive's mind, the means for promoting virtue discussed by Professor Christie Davies will attract his scorn. Respectability is today derided as small-mindedness, a way of scaling down virtue for the unheroic, the unimaginative. That, says Professor Davies, is why it is so effective a way of attaching large numbers of ordinary, morally unheroic people to good habits. If the task is to attach the vast majority of ordinary people to virtuous behaviour, then what is needed is an incentive that will work for the many, not just for a few saints. Respectability is that incentive. In particular the fear of the shame involved in its loss kept many working class and lower middle class families sober, industrious, and intact. Few people can be successful. Almost everyone can be respectable.

The success of respectability is proven over the century that lasted from the mid-nineteenth to the mid-twentieth. Derided as hypocritical, smug, and narrow by today's progressive thinkers, it is much less a source of order than it was. And the crime and social decay of late twentieth century Britain and America are the result of the subversion of respectability. For those progressive thinkers have nothing to put in its place as a source of order.

Respectability and its key component, trust, have been driven from the professions, especially law and teaching. From the right, the pressure to get results, success, from the left, egalitarianism, have undermined respectability so that lawyers now are objects of scorn and humour, not admiration and trust.

Approbation is to children what respectability is to adults, a workable way of attaching them to virtuous behaviour. It offends against progressive ideas of equality: it singles children out for approval. And it, like respectability, often cannot give reasons for its judgements, beyond 'because that is the way we do things here'. But it works. To abandon it is highly dangerous.

Repression and inhibition

For over half a century repression has been thought to be damaging. In popular culture men and women are depicted as having needs, the denial of which is dangerous. The popular phrases are coming to terms with oneself, coming out, being happy with oneself, being true to oneself. Denying and blocking such needs is unhealthy. Yet, as Professor Rychlak reminds us, repression, under its nineteenth century name, self-control, was once thought a good thing. It was once thought not only desirable, but necessary for social order. This change in reputation has come about largely from the influence of two psychological schools, Freudianism and Behaviourism. Both base themselves on a Newtonian view of science, the Behaviourists enthusiastically, Freud in response to the urgings of his colleagues and more ambivalently. This view of science defines cause, and therefore the explanations science may seek, in ways which do not admit of human agency, intention, or purpose. They thus demoralise action. Freudianism therefore presents individuals as being repressed or blocked by internal dynamics over which they have little understanding or control. Behaviourism presents the individual as being controlled by external stimuli.

Yet a considered look at the Freudian thinking on repression shows a role for understanding and purpose is possible and hence an admission of responsibility. 'What we call "character" [is not just the result of internal or external forces but] is germinated in the graceful acceptance of life's negative reinforcements, as well as overcoming them though personal effort. [Human] agents also reap the benefits of praise and satisfaction when decisions are successful. Finally, agents know that for an orderly and satisfying personal life, as well as promoting tranquillity in social affairs, a degree of self-suppression (conscious "repression") is not only inevitable but highly desirable'.

Leadership and trust

There is an increasing recognition that the last decade or so has witnessed a failure to understand and sustain traditional institutions. In Britain there are clear signs of disintegration in key traditional institutions, notably the Monarchy, Parliament, local government, and public services. The disintegrating forces are many: socialism, the 1960s celebration of questioning authority, the end of the certainties of the Cold War, and the undermining of nation states by supra-national institutions, separatist tendencies, and a global economy. And last, but by no means least, the misapplication of short-term meritocratic requirements to traditional institutions.

Dr. Dandeker argues that this is especially the case in the requirement that institutions behave like occupations and replace traditional virtues such as loyalty, personal moral integrity, and life-time service with cost-effectiveness and other outcome measures. This misapplication has done damage both to particular services, such as the military, and to society as a whole.

The military is an ideal type of a traditional institution and its special position in society fits it not only to act as a warning against disintegrative forces, but as an example of integrating ones. And the key quality in integration in both the military and society is trust, which is the basis of moral authority.

Fear—of pain and shame

Thomas Hobbes identified the powers of lust and repulsion, or 'appetite and aversion', as the pillars of human conduct. In so doing, he balanced fear and love or friendship as effective motivations among human beings. At the same time, however, Hobbes made clear that appetite was narrower than love, focusing mainly on the sensation of pleasure, while aversion was focused mainly on the sensation of pain (and thus, rightly, called fear). Hobbesian materialism introduced to the modern ear the possibility that human conduct could be regulated with resort to the powerful positive and negative forces of pleasure and pain.

Regarding pain, however, as Professor William Allen explains, an interesting thing occurred. The fear which disposes men to avoid painful exigencies, once it is understood only in material and not in social terms, becomes a much narrower construct than would have operated in the sons of a Brutus in ancient Rome. When Brutus surrendered his sons to the laws of the state, stifling every paternal affection, he provided a powerful lesson to every other father and son. He did this because the pain of shame was a more powerful motivation than the pain of losing his sons to execution. In those earlier days, fear was a much bigger word, the kind that caused an Antigone to respond to an Ismene that execution at the hands of the state terrified her far less than the shame of infidelity to her family. Ismene was afraid, and called cowardly by her sister. Antigone, however, was no less afraid, afraid to dishonour her family.

The fear which motivates upright conduct has no share in the fear of pain, for often enough it fosters a willingness to endure pain in order to avoid shame. Since the age of materialism has spread so generally throughout the world, however, it is almost only the fear of pain which is felt by individuals. A result is that social conduct is largely unrestrained precisely in those areas where fear alone could operate as a restraint. For example, schoolchildren in urban areas rarely fear their parents learning of their delinquencies (as once was true) so much as they fear falling victim to their fellow delinquents. They will accordingly arm themselves and shoot. Peer pressure is often evoked in explanation of much youth behaviour. It is the case, however, that peer pressure would be but an impoverished version of the system of moral restraints in a mature society. Do the young truly respond from a fear of losing the respect of their peers, or do they respond in a world characterised by a vacuum of respect? In fact what looks like peer pressure is nothing but the line of least resistance consistent with personal tastes for pleasures and pains. The only means to alter this pattern is to re-establish the vigorous operation of a fear of shame. Some modern Brutus must demonstrate for his weaker-willed fellows what it means to be dishonoured by one's sons, in order for a healthy, social fear to recover its power to guide human conduct.

Loving the good

Faced with moral collapse (as today) it is always tempting to call for a return to a law ethic backed by force of some of the above kinds, as this seems at first sight the most effective way of ensuring moral behaviour and of opposing the choice-based, expressivist ethics which have so patently failed to guide people. Such fear must be a component of any moral society, but Linda Woodhead queries whether this is the best and the *primary* way to counter the loss of virtue.

At first sight, fear is a prominent way Christianity has traditionally used to engender virtue. Threats are not absent from the Bible: in the Old Testament it is clear what will happen to Israel if her people turn from the Lord; disaster will follow. Jesus continues this theme in His teaching and speaks clearly of the wrath which awaits those who reject the Good News. But the important point is that, in both the Jewish and Christian traditions, God is primarily a God of mercy, not judgement. He is a God who offers blessings to His people. Punishments and curses follow from rejecting God's mercy but the punishment is not a threat to get people to turn to God. They should turn to Him out of love; out of the recognition that He and His creation are good and worthy of love.

The Christian ethic, then, is based on love not fear. And though laws are central in the tradition, the love is not for the laws as laws, but for the goods which they safeguard. (Do not blaspheme because God is good; do not kill because human life is good; do not commit adultery because marriage is good; do not steal because property is good.) The reason for obedience to the laws is not fear, but love for the goods which the laws protect.

So Christian moral formation takes place in a number of linked ways, all of them bound up with its communal existence. First, by instructing people about what is good, and about the hierarchy of goods; a vision of life and the world as a whole. Secondly, by constantly meditating on the good in liturgy and trying to conform oneself to it. Thirdly, by offering forgiveness and the chance to begin again when people fall short of the good. And, fourthly, by bearing witness to the good in lives and communities. The church is not just the place where moral instruction takes place, it is the place where goods become present, where God comes to earth and where love, forgiveness, generosity, peace, and justice are shown in people's relations with one another; a community of goods.

There is a frightening reluctance on the part of modern people to acknowledge any goods. It has become unfashionable to celebrate anything except the most abstract ideals: justice, equality, self-knowledge, freedom. To claim that the nation, the family, property, even human life, are goods is to call down accusations of arrogance and naivety.

This loss of belief in and love for the good and for goods is the most dangerous feature of contemporary society. People can be made to act well by obeying laws out of fear, but this can only ever be a partial solution. It is too fragile and contingent to be anything more. True morality only exists where people love the good and when their actions flow from this love. We need communities of goods if we are to survive.

The juxtaposition of the Allen and Woodhead chapters is deliberate. The reader must judge for himself whether the fear Allen values and the love of which Woodhead speaks are contradictions or part of the same dynamic of virtue. What is not in doubt is that both involve a readiness to sacrifice and to suffer. Whatever it is that must be done to reclaim virtue and order, it will hurt.

But is civic order possible in the typical modern community, the city?

It is no longer controversial but commonplace to recognise that America and Britain are going through some sort of social crisis. To one set of people, including many politicians, bureaucrats, and social scientists, this can be solved by government. Better government, better policing, new policies can substitute for people behaving better. Others recognise that the regaining of social order means that individuals must become better behaved, at least in those behaviours which affect others. They divide behaviour into public and private and, while allowing freedom in the private sphere, call for more responsibility in the public sphere.

Professor Ross Lence asks whether even this goes far enough. He suggests that two more steps are necessary. The first is to recognise that true virtue cannot be limited to whatever may happen to have public consequences. Social order depends on virtue *per se*, not just such virtues as can be supposed to have various consequences for others. Second, and even more radically, he argues that even the restoration of thorough-going virtue is not enough.

Order requires an environment in which virtue can prosper. The old rural community had order because men lived close to each other, knew each other, and lived in friendship. The modern city has none of the conditions in which virtue can prosper. It provides freedom to the point of licence and anonymity to the point of irresponsibility. Quite simply, if we want the security of community we may have to give up the modern city. For it no longer has those characteristics which Plato considered conditions of virtue. Los Angeles is not Athens.

The trouble is that the city, as well as being the source of uncivil behaviour, is also the source of the great achievements of Western civilization. The material wealth, the arts, sophisticated 'society' are the glorious achievements of the city. And men like them. They may yearn for the security of the country in their speeches, but their feet show their true priorities and they take them to the city, its freedoms, anonymity, pleasures, and culture.

That, says Professor Lence, is the final cost of a return to virtue and order, the giving up of the achievements and pleasures of the city. Men are unlikely to pay that price. The crisis in order will continue.

CHAPTER 1

The Necessity
of
Guilt and Shame:

Dostoevsky's Warning to the Modern World

Michael Aeschliman

1920s–1990s: The repudiation of shame in the name of self-gratification

The revolt against what are called 'Victorian values' commenced in earnest, in the sense that it reached 'critical mass', in the 1920s and, despite a sobering period from 1929 until the end of the Korean War around 1953, was renewed with great vigour in the 1960s. The one set of emotions and reactions against which the anti-Victorian liberators set themselves more than any other was the spectrum of feeling ranging from embarrassment and shame to guilt. These came more and more to be depicted as neuroses, 'hang-ups', and emotional deprivations or perversions. Despite a powerful anti-hedonistic satire such as Aldous Huxley's *Brave New World* (1932)—one of the great books of the century—and the lucubrations of the late Freud, the growing consensus of high-brow and mid-brow opinion since the 1920s has been distinctly in the direction of 'the Playboy philosophy'. Self-exhibition, self-expression, and immediate gratification are endlessly promoted and praised, while inhibition, repression, and sublimation are deplored or mocked. Platonism, Puritanism, and Victorianism have become interchangeably abusive and derogatory terms.[1]

When Tennyson wrote in 1872 of the Western moral tradition that 'it will bind thee by such vows as is a shame / A man should not be bound by, yet the which / No man can keep' (*Gareth and Lynette*), he was reiterating a central paradox at least as old as St. Paul's Epistle to the Romans—that we see and approve the good, but, being weak-willed, often follow the bad, and feel shame and guilt when we do; and that knowing and dealing with our moral

3

deficiencies—repenting and amending them—is the perennial, serious, universal, and life-long business of being or becoming a mature human being.

Of course, embarrassment, shame, and guilt are extremely unpleasant emotions and in some cases crippling ones. An excessive sense of them certainly can lead to low self-esteem, pervasive melancholy or depression, and emotional misery. That Puritanical Protestantism and Augustinian Catholicism have sometimes led to emotional masochism, terror, grief, and despair is not to be doubted, perhaps especially in the tradition of Calvinism, with its emphasis on the radical depravity and lostness of the helpless, unredeemed sinner. Romantic assertions of the radical goodness, sufficiency, or autonomy of the self were often dramatic and extreme rejections of traditional Calvinist pessimism about human nature: Rousseau and Pestalozzi in Switzerland; Burns and Byron in Scotland; Emerson, Thoreau, Whitman, and Parker in New England and New York. Whitman was unashamed and unembarrassed to 'celebrate' himself, even the polymorphous, promiscuous, democratic drifter-aesthete and self-promoter that he was.[2]

But self-fulfilment has no answer to soaring crime rates, illegitimacy, and civil chaos

By the late 19th century, among the intelligentsia, 'progressive' social attitudes were clearly in the ascendant over the older austerity of Anglo-American Protestantism, as well as over the similar and more culturally marginal Catholicism of Irish, Italian, and Polish immigrants to America. The sequel has been briefly sketched above. But given our increasing social disorder and breakdown—reflected in violent crime, illegitimacy, divorce, decreasing literacy and civic awareness, and a more and more poisonous and perverse cultural milieu—the effects of naked hedonism and of shameless and guiltless models for behaviour have begun to worry not only parents and police but also politicians and even some intellectuals.

Is a post-theistic 'world of incessant autobiography' (C. S. Lewis) where many people have jettisoned the emotional and moral baggage of embarrassment, shame, and guilt really capable of sustaining or even tolerating a decent social order for much longer without destroying it altogether? Liberal utilitarianism has never been in worse shape in terms of credibility and efficacy than it is today, 200 years after its first great political triumph in the French Revolution. Neil Coughlan has argued that John Dewey is 'the philosopher *par excellence* of American liberalism' because 'he shares with it the root conviction that we can have both self-defined self-fulfilment and social justice for all'.[3] But these two values have proved incapable of being harmonized and what Christopher Lasch calls 'the culture of Narcissism' has undermined or overwhelmed the imperatives and even the intelligibility of civic obligation and social deference, especially in America.

One cannot laud 'community' and refuse to admit limitations to self-gratification

The 'historical fact appears to be', Quentin Anderson wrote recently, 'that American intellectuals show a reluctance or inability to admit that any limitation of the goal of "self-fulfilment" is implied by membership in the community', though we can now sadly add all other professions and social strata to the number of those who display such reluctance or inability.[4]

The social, civic consciousness and its imperatives have proved to be more fragile and evanescent than Anglo-American progressives, from Bentham to Laski and Dewey and Hook, ever realised or suspected. Morally inverted, in Michael Polanyi's phrase, Western radicals now assert the most extravagant claims to personal liberation, radical pluralism, and social obligation *all at once*, apparently not realising that these three are lethal to one another, and that if Nietzschean Deconstruction is consistently used to destroy or debunk the residual momentum of the orthodox Western moral tradition, it provides an open field for Social Darwinism and libertarian capitalism at their most naked. Nietzsche was not a left-wing thinker and had only contempt for the 'herd' and utilitarian ethics. Humanitarian feelings are fluid and undependable: as Philip Rieff has said, behind the Hippie stands the Hell's Angel. From Bernard Mandeville to Ayn Rand is a straight line, and if the libertarian has no time or tolerance for embarrassment, shame, or guilt, neither does he have time for social-welfare ideas or agencies. Between the naked self-assertion and self-love of Ayn Rand's 'virtue of selfishness' and the radical Narcissism and exhibitionism of the 'Rock' culture that engulfs our young there is not ultimately a dime's worth of moral difference, though one wears a pin-striped suit.

Yet a sense of shame, albeit a confused one, persists

Yet the residual momentum of older social and moral ideas and habits is still with us, however weak and fragile. There is a widely recognised moral common sense or 'Natural Law' which has been the heart and essence of civilisation wherever it has prevailed *as such*, as opposed to tyranny or the mere anarchic aggregate of competitive selves. In reflective moments, we still say to our children, and ourselves, 'what if everyone did that?' and 'that's no way to treat people' and 'he (or I, or you) ought to be ashamed of himself (or myself, yourself)'. Despite the sinister symbiosis of the post-moral radical and the post-moral libertarian, whose collaborative ascendency is now apparent in the arts, movies, television, advertising, glossy magazines, and the rock culture, there is still a wide pool of unease about the promotion and admiration of brassy, unembarrassed arrogance. No reflective person with any degree of moral awareness can doubt that naked impudence and insolent self-interest are lethal to the *res publica* of the West on whose moral capital and momentum we continue to live and depend for whatever decency, dignity, and security remain.

Yet such is the 'deconstructed' or decadent state of our culture and society that *words* such as 'decency' and 'dignity', along with others such as 'duty', 'good manners', and 'reverence' tend to die on our lips or to evoke an immediately ironic reaction in others. And if the language of the virtues evokes an undermining irony, so too does the implicit disapproval in the very names of wrong-doing and wrong-doers: how credible are words such as 'scoundrel', 'villain', 'sinner', or 'wrong-doer'? In Alasdair MacIntyre's formulation, we live in an age 'after virtue', and apparently 'after vice' as well. Radicalism, relativism, and pluralism, fed from numerous sources, have undermined the intelligibility and credibility of moral language itself.[5] Our decadence is not only social but also linguistic, and at all social and cultural levels. Linguistically, virtue has lost its lustre; we cannot taste the linguistic truth of the truism; the dialect of the tribe has become polluted.

In the 19th century, confidently intoxicated with the religion of inevitable, collective, linear progress, few foresaw such a development in the 20th century, or the wars and social cataclysms from 1914 on that helped stimulate and create our pervasive and free-floating sense of irony about all moral realities. A few far-sighted souls saw the falsehood of the idea of inevitable collective progress: the Popes, John Henry Newman, Søren Kierkegaard, the historian Jakob Burckhardt, Fyodor Dostoevsky, and, intermittently, the poet Baudelaire. But the linguistic corruption in its full stature was foreseen only, I think, by Dostoevsky.

Dostoevsky, the prophet of the loss of virtue and the coming shameless society

How and why did Dostoevsky prophesy this and what did he do about it?

As deeply as Nietzsche, Dostoevsky understood that nihilism was coming to be the cultural milieu in which modern people would more and more live, or, to use the later formulation of Flannery O'Connor, the gas they would inevitably have to breathe. Unlike Nietzsche, whose tragic and pro-

6

found mind oscillated wildly between the roles of evangelist, witness, and martyr to this nihilism, Dostoevsky steadily and deeply hated and opposed it. But like Nietzsche and Baudelaire, he understood it experientially, existentially, from the inside out, from within the skin, so to speak. It was the darkening shadow over his age, advancing largely by that pervasive undermining and corruption of moral language.

Like Nietzsche, Dostoevsky knew that secularisation, liberalism, and utilitarianism were inadequate and ultimately unbelievable replacements for the Christian faith and world view—that at their highest levels of belief, loyalty, and practice, people will not accept or live by merely heuristic truths, to use Philip Rieff's formulation.[6] No writer of the world before 1914 saw these issues with such hallucinatory clarity and foreboding.

Dostoevsky saw how reason, science, and 'progress' might undermine the credibility of ethics and social order with it

The liberal, rational, progressive mind of the 19th century assumed a happy congruity between science, reason, ethics, and language, all collaborating and conducing to steady and rapid improvement of the whole human species. It assumed that by walking straight forward by the light of the sciences, human beings would mount into the air, as Simone Weil was later to put it. But like Kierkegaard and Nietzsche, Dostoevsky was aware of the ontological density and depth of human nature, for good and ill. The cold, value-free language and attitude of the sciences might well destroy the credibility of ethics altogether, and finally assimilate the human person to mere nature. Mass murder was to be industrialised, and lampshades made of human skin, by the world's most scientifically advanced people.

For satirizing both the simplistic liberal progressivism and the ruthless revolutionary progressivism of his day, Dostoevsky was widely hated during his life, banned by the triumphant Marxists after 1917, and neglected, ignored, or attacked by liberals ever since. Of course, he has been a profound inspiration to major writers such as Gissing, T. S. Eliot, Claudel, Camus, and several of his own countrymen such as Solzhenitzyn, Sinyavsky, and Mandelstam, as well as to theologians such as Barth, Lubac, and Balthasar and several generations of Russian Orthodox religious thinkers.[7] However, he has also been plausibly but ultimately misleadingly dragooned, along with Kierkegaard, into the company of atheistic existentialists such as Jean-Paul Sartre.

The linking of Dostoevsky with the absurdists is plausible because he clearly understood and convincingly depicted the incidents and even periods of every person's life that are or seem to be sheerly anomalous. Concentrating on them, modernist, absurdist or 'heterodox' irony became common in French literature in the late 18th century. It is incipient in Voltaire and Diderot, ascendant in Laclos, and at flood-tide in the Marquis de Sade. By the 19th century it was widespread in Balzac, Flaubert, and Stendhal. It dominates modern literature—think of the title of Kundera's novel, *The Unbearable Lightness of Being*—and much modern criticism too. Deconstructionism is systematically ironic and anarchic *vis à vis* the central 'logocentric' heritage of Western literature, philosophy, and religion, from Plato and the Prophets to T. S. Eliot. God has been rejected for tenure, and His mockers chosen instead.

Dostoevsky both experienced and rejected the nihilism of modern life

As well as Stendhal or Nietzsche, Dostoevsky has experienced, knows, and can depict this feeling and belief that 'everything that is solid melts into the air' of modernity (Marx's phrase), that life is ultimately anomalous and ironic, a fraud or an accident, a tissue of relativities, a 'tale told by an idiot', that there is no moral framework, core, or 'point' to reality, that 'we all live in a yellow submarine'. After attending a performance of Alfred Jarry's absurdist play *Ubu Roi* early in our century, William Butler Yeats saw in it the shape of things to come, in art and life: 'after us [comes] the Savage God', he wrote.[8] The savage god of absurdism and nihilism now profitably populates our television screens and radio broadcasts, and strides unashamedly through our streets. Dostoevsky foresaw and depicted 'the savage god' and the milieu of ironic nihilism in which he lived: in Smerdyakov, old Fyodor, and intermittently in Ivan in *The Brothers Karamazov*; in Raskolnikov in *Crime and Punishment*; in Stavrogin, Peter Verchovensky, and intermittently in Kirilov, among many others in *The Devils*; and persistently in 'the Underground Man'. Whether this ultimately ironic and anomalous view of life issues in libertine cynicism and aesthetic immoralism (as in the Marquis de Sade or Stendhal) or bitter, lethal, or glib revolutionary radicalism (as in Marxism or today's Deconstructionism), or in oscillations between or combinations of the two, Dostoevsky *knows* it, and he depicts it in an unforgettable gallery of deranged or sinister types, some of whom he even loves and pities (e.g., Kirilov in *The Devils*), but all of whom he disapproves of, satirises, and deplores.[9]

For although he employs this heterodox irony and concedes, even asserts, its existential cogency and accuracy for much of our individual and common life, he constantly contrasts and undermines it by juxtaposing to it

another kind or conception of irony that is the tool of his ultimate and pervasive orientation toward the Good, toward the Christian Logos, within and
beyond both self and society.[10] This 'orthodox' irony is logocentric in its
uses and aims, and the modernity and subtle but insistent mastery of his use
of it 'lifts him', as John Updike has said, 'into the empyrean of Western literature, into that small circle of writers who have appreciably enlarged
[human] self-knowledge'.[11]

Goodness as the essence of self-knowledge and social order

This orthodox irony is a kind of *basso continuo* in all of Dostoevsky's writing. However intermittently confused or perverted and incipiently tragic or
pathetic life is, in this ultimate perspective the Good is believed, praised,
and vindicated. Orthodox irony is Providential, it serves the Good, it 'justi-
fies God's ways to man'. The working aesthetic of Dostoevsky's writing
serves and implicates moral reality as *reality*. We are made to 'see feelingly',
and what we are drawn to see and say—if we read aright—is that the Good
exists within us but also independently of us, that we are indebted to it and
ought to be grateful for it, and that it is to be praised and cherished as the
essence and source of self-knowledge, sanity, and social order—of 'decent
Godly order'.[12]

Shame and embarrassment most necessary to lead individuals to virtue and wisdom

The vicarious imaginative experiences through which Dostoevsky puts his
attentive reader are often negative in the sense of being painful ones.
Ignorance, folly, weakness, self-delusion, wickedness, vice, and sin are
perennial temptations, and individuals ought always to contend with them
to mitigate them. Self-knowledge is never once and for all earned and
achieved, but is rather a process of constant growth, and Dostoevsky's use
of orthodox irony is a kind of moral hygiene which the modern world badly
needs.

This moral hygiene often employs the emotions of embarrassment,
shame, and guilt as tools, as the intimate and necessary forms of personal
suffering—for characters and readers—that can lead to virtue, wisdom,
charity and, sometimes, even to sanctity. In Dostoevsky's ironic depiction of
various modes of modern 'liberation' from religion, conventional ethics,
deference, manners, and social constraint, he carries the anarchic (read
nowadays: 'Deconstructionist') project to its logical outcome: a world of
venomously post-moral selves, snakes in a pit who are unburdened by

allegedly superstitious residues such as embarrassment, shame, or guilt; a world of audacious radicals or libertarians (Marxists or Nietzscheans) who have effaced from themselves and those influenced by them the inherited, historically transmitted sense of the 'image of God', the voice of conscience (*vox conscientiae*), that civilizes us, however imperfectly. The thrill-seeking aesthete, boldly nihilistic intellectual, or revolutionary zealot (often phases or moods in the life of the same person), is an incipient criminal or devil, possessed by what Dostoevsky calls in *The Devils* 'the demon of irony'.[13] Against this heterodox, corrosive, demoralising irony—now so pervasive in modern literature and life—Dostoevsky opposes the 'logocentric' or orthodox irony that is rooted in moral experience itself and which is for him ultimately truer to the facts of human history and of human and divine nature, and which vindicates the ethics of the Natural Law and gives needed succour and solace to the anxious moral self.

The horror of a life without shame: the inability to feel good and evil

Dostoevsky's corrosively self-conscious 'Underground Man', taking secular rationalism to its ultimate limit, shows how without firm moral foundations it stultifies itself; how relativistic, scientistic, and deterministic thinking assimilate mind, will, and person to the chains of causal necessity, and undermine or obliterate moral common sense and the specifically human essence: 'Thus it would follow, as the result of hyperconsciousness', he says, 'that one is not to blame for being a scoundrel, as though that were any consolation to the scoundrel once he has come to realise that he actually is a scoundrel'.[14]

In the dialectical oscillations of their minds, spirits, and beliefs, Dostoevsky's characters reveal perhaps more poignantly and impressively than those of any other writer the very dynamics or phenomenology of consciousness itself—the naked thinking mind and the naked feeling heart. His aesthetic aristocrat Stavrogin lives out and comments on the post-moral freedom of nihilism, the decadent liberty of the void, the absurd fruit of relativism:

> I neither know nor feel good or evil and . . . I have not only lost any sense of it, but there is neither good nor evil (which pleased me), and . . . it is just a prejudice; [and] I can be free from any prejudice, but . . . once I attain that degree of freedom I am done for.[15]

This is the post-moral freedom of the devil, the lunatic, the terrorist, the gangster, the human predator, and Dostoevsky saw it as lethal to self and society.

This novel, *The Devils*, as Edward Wasiolek has said, 'is about men who have forgotten who and why they are. It is both fact and prophecy'.[16] It hauntingly depicts and prophesies not only the Bolshevik Revolution and the morally-inverted fanatics who made it, but also more generally the deracinated radical mind of our century and our moment, a mind at once relativistic and moralistic, as Michael Polanyi was to argue after watching the Bolsheviks themselves at work and talking with them.[17]

Society without manners and embarrassment

So acute is Dostoevsky's insight into human dynamics, so sharp his sense in the mid-19th century of the disintegration to come in our own, that it is impossible, as Nadezhda Mandelstam says, 'to think of him as a mere "novelist" '.[18] The chapter 'At Virginsky's' in Part Two of *The Devils* is one of the great satires we have on what social aggregations without decent prejudices, good manners, and elementary religious piety really will be—groups of venomously self-assertive individuals, shameless in their rudeness, unembarrassed in their contradictory but despotic moral denunciations and calls for revolutionary blood-letting and revenge. Hating allegedly primitive 'prejudices' such as honour and piety, the turbulent radicals assault and scorn not only all inherited social forms and virtues, but each other as well. There is, after all, no basis for honour or deference among relativists, unless it be the masochistic deference to the most despotic, audacious, and shameless will—to the Lenin or Hitler, the Al Capone or Charles Manson. The depiction of the breathtakingly vicious spite with which these radicals treat each other is a masterpiece of orthodox irony in service to the moral imagination, showing that without the elementary practice of Natural-Law virtues, there is actually no basis for *any* social bond.

Humaneness only a habit: it can be lost and is disappearing in American cities

During the Second World War, Paul Valéry was to write that 'civilisations are mortal', but three-quarters of a century earlier Dostoevsky had written that 'humaneness is only a habit, a product of civilisation. It may completely disappear'.[19]

Over large stretches of terrain for substantial stretches of time in our century it has disappeared, and in many American cities—not to speak of South American, African, or Chinese ones—it has evaporated, leaving people to cower among squalid ruins and terrifying social conditions. The 19th-century optimists were wrong about the human future; Dostoevsky was right. In 1873 he wrote derisively of utopian expectations: 'this chimerical frenzy, all this gloom and horror which is being prepared for humankind under the guise of regeneration and resurrection'.[20] His narrator in *The Devils* (1871) first listens to and then interrupts and mocks the progressive scenario and utopian dream conjured up by the tragic revolutionary fanatic, Kirilov:

> 'Then there will be a new life [Kirilov says], a new man, everything will be new. Then history will be divided into two parts: from the gorilla to the annihilation of God, and from the annihilation of God to . . .'
> 'To the gorilla?'[21]

Shame as the awareness of responsibility: essential to civilised life

The capacity rightly to feel embarrassment, shame, and guilt for bad conduct, to wish to amend that conduct and to behave so as not to suffer such internal and external reproach, is of the essence of Dostoevsky's Christian wisdom, the essence of being a person and not a gorilla. Very much in Dostoevsky's spirit, his admirer and our contemporary Nadezhda Mandelstam has written that 'The feeling of sinfulness is the basic "wealth of man" . . . because the awareness of the actual responsibility for one's own destiny and that of others is precisely what makes [a person] spiritually free and brings him back in touch with life'.[22]

CHAPTER 2

After Virtue, Law

F. H. Buckley

Changes in law have weakened the private virtues which sustain a well-ordered society

This chapter examines the world we lost when *Ancien Régime* virtues were discarded for modern values, when honour gave way to self-discovery, and loyalty to personal growth.[1] I shall discuss how modern American legal norms have degraded traditional social norms and weakened private virtues, then suggest why this might have happened.

Morality not just a list of virtues but a collection of ways for attaching people to virtues, such as shame

When I read law, 20 years ago, the materials I studied bore a family resemblance to the common law of Blackstone's *Commentaries.* These similarities are largely erased from the materials I teach today, at a modern American law school. In part, this difference reflects the conservative legal training I received. More importantly, the law has changed in ways that Blackstone would not recognise. In Blackstone's day, the common law was less intrusive and more closely in accord with common-sense morality. Changes in the law since then have plausibly weakened the private virtues which bind us together in a well-ordered society.

The new legal order benefits the legal profession. Expanding law's empire increases a lawyer's billable hours, and this may in part explain the new legal regime. In addition, changes in legal norms respond to changes in social ones, with lawyers and judges reflecting contemporary social values. Through a continuous feedback, the new legal norms reinforce social norms.

Law, misdirected, can depart from and undermine virtues and moral sanctions

Legal penalties usefully reinforce social sanctions for serious offenses. We should not wish to invite a murderer for tea, but do not expect that this provides an adequate deterrence for murder. Because of this, murder is a crime as well as a social lapse. A well-ordered system of laws, therefore, represents an advance over the state of nature. One the other hand, laws may subvert valuable social norms when the two are inconsistent. Thus, modern legal regimes promote liberal social causes such as feminism, gay rights, and abortion, which are very much at variance with traditional social norms. For example, private agreements between husband and wife not to divorce are illegal. Many states prohibit discrimination by landlords on the basis of marital status, and two brothers in Massachusetts recently found themselves sued by the state Attorney General because they refused on religious grounds to rent an apartment to an unmarried couple.[2] More recently, the U.S. Supreme Court has upheld an injunction on pro-life protests, which might perhaps include prayer vigils, within 36 feet of the entrance to an abortion clinic.[3]

I do not deny that the common law has always taken sides on private or moral issues. In Blackstone's day, for example, blasphemy was a crime, and the practice of Catholicism severely curtailed.[4] What is different today, however, is the divergence between contemporary legal values and common-sense morality. Criminalising private virtue undermines social norms and subverts the authority of their oracles. By contrast, 18th-century law sought to strengthen common-sense morality by privileging a dominant religion.

I also admit that legal innovations are at times to be preferred to common-sense moral rules. Common-sense morality is not infallible, after all. If legal rules should reflect moral values, then lawyers are not bound to adopt every contemporary social norm. For example, the civil rights laws which granted full legal capacity to blacks—the right to vote, to sue, and to hold property—were controversial when passed, but without doubt were benign.

I do claim, however, that lawyers should exercise great prudence in departing from common-sense moral rules, and that prudence is no longer much prized by lawyers. Instead, lawyers have assumed the role of a priestly class, with a privileged knowledge of the good. They are more apt to regard common-sense moral rules as the product of false consciousness than as a source of knowledge about the good.[5] Their contempt for social norms invites the layman's contempt for legal rules, thereby weakening a bulwark of morality.

The collapse of public safety in U.S. cities: the growth of crime and coarseness

The distinction between sacred and secular is lost on the liberal. If there is a need for spiritual meaning, then a Hillary Clinton will seek to provide it. In this way, modern states attempt to do that which they cannot, while omitting to do that which they can. Nowhere is the failure of modern governments more evident than in the collapse of public safety, particularly in large American cities.

The costs of crime are borne by all Americans, even those who never encounter a mugger. Such costs include the monies spent on the criminal justice system and on private police services. However, the most important cost of crime is the destruction of the amenities of civilized life: the ability to walk about without fear, the abandonment of cities for barren suburbs of cul-de-sacs, the long commutes along crowded highways, the closing of neighbourhood shops, the surrender of city parks and gardens, and the coarseness of everyday life. Not surprisingly, such costs are borne more heavily by women and children than by men: this is not, after all, a particularly gentlemanly generation.

Criminal sanctions currently too weak

The increase in crime may plausibly be attributed to a relaxation of criminal sanctions. In the past, criminal sanctions were considerably more severe. Nowadays, sentences are lighter, and with generous parole provisions, criminals spend only 40 per cent of their sentenced time in prison.[6] From an economic perspective, crime is now a more attractive career opportunity. In addition, social norms are strengthened when strong legal sanctions reinforce social ones, and weakened when the legal sanction is relaxed.

This point was brought home to me in a very forceful way when I was ten years old, and embarked on a week-long crime spree. With a group of friends, I raided the gardens of neighbours at night to steal peas and carrots. For a few days, our parents let us get away with it. They must have found it vastly amusing that we ate by night the vegetables we pushed from our plates by day. But soon they decided that enough was enough. Other children were simply told to stop it. However, my father was a friend of the local RCMP constable, who came to our house in full dress uniform to give me a lecture on crime and punishment. Quaking with fear, I told him I would stop stealing vegetables from other people's gardens, and I am proud to report that I have kept my promise.

The incident taught me a deeper lesson. I learned that, no matter how secure one might seem to be, it was always one short step to perdition. One could work hard, have a successful career, a wonderful family, and be a respected member of one's community, but if you took that one little step in the wrong direction, it would not count for anything. Afterwards, you could try to hide from it, change your name, move to a new state, and you'd still end up, like Paul Muni, back on the chain gang.

Teach these lessons today, and one might be sued for child abuse. Pity, for they serve a very useful purpose. Through them, we learned that there were no free rides, that grace was free but not cheap, and that the trick was to avoid the first mis-step.

Criminal sanctions may be excessive, if they might proscribe innocuous behaviour, or frighten one from taking up valuable business opportunities. Criminals will also be over-deterred unless some fresh starts are accorded. For example, one who commits an assault may have little incentive not to kill if the penalty and probability of detection are the same in both cases. At present, however, sentences would appear to be relatively lax, and far from the threshold of over-deterrence.

Crime is also reduced when the probability of detection increases. An increased police presence in the inner city would also reduce crime rates. What does not appear to work, however, is legislation which focuses on the 'root causes' of crime, consigning billions of dollars to social workers, criminal justice centres, and community-based programmes. Such efforts appear to do little other than transfer scarce resources to a criminal justice bureaucracy.

Legal imperialism threatens social norms: the expansion of tort law and wasteful litigation

On returning home, Goldsmith's Traveller realised 'How small, of all that human hearts endure, That part which laws or kings can cause or cure'.[7] What he meant, of course, was that law cannot aspire to satisfy one's deepest wants. For a modern lawyer, however, the poem stands as an indictment of 18th-century legal systems. If a want had gone uncured, there should have been a law.

It is easy to parody the hubris of modern lawyers. However, the expansion of legal rules in the United States into every nook and cranny of everyday behaviour is a very serious matter. A modern traveller wanders through this country casually amassing causes of action, for which it is only too easy to persuade a lawyer to litigate on a contingency fee basis.[8] Horrible examples abound, but I rather like the following. A patient sued a hospital over an allergic reaction to a drug, and claimed special damages because, as a professional psychic, she was subsequently unable to conduct séances; the voices no longer spoke to her. The judge instructed the jury to ignore this claim, but it came back 45 minutes later with an award of $986,000. The judge ordered a new trial, and four years later the litigation continued.[9] The expansion of tort law results in wasteful litigation which benefits lawyers but no one much else. Another source of waste is legal uncertainty as to substantive law and remedy, since no one will litigate over a sure thing.

When every slight can be litigated, damage is separated from shame

Apart from these costs, however, legal imperialism weakens the social sanctions which deter wrongful conduct in regimes with a thinner set of laws. When every slight can be litigated, then the principal remedy for any wrong will be found in a court of law, and not in the good opinion of one's fellow subjects. When this happens, a breach will occasion an award of damages, but not a sense of shame. Having compensated the victim, the wrongdoer will feel that he has paid his debt in full.

Because of this, common law courts have traditionally refused to enforce non-commercial promises made between family members. For example, a brother's promise to give a house to his sister if she moved to his part of the state was held to be revocable in an 1845 Alabama decision.[10] In nearly all such cases, family sentiment provides an adequate sanction for wrongful breach. Granting family members standing to sue would weaken such bonds, and result in a smaller number of family promises.

This is not an argument for a return to the state of nature. In a commercial context, we should be a great deal poorer if the parties to a bargain were unable to seek redress for breach, as in Russia today. But we should be wary of extending law's empire beyond such bounds, to enforce family promises or dates for a high school prom, or to permit recovery in tort for trivial harms.

Excessive legal remedies subvert fortitude: claims for 'emotional distress'

An excessive grant of legal remedies may thus be seen to weaken social norms of fellowship, trust, and honour. In addition, the grant of a remedy for trivial wrongs places a premium on whining, and subverts the virtue of fortitude.[11]

Common law courts have traditionally been sceptical of claims for emotional distress. In general, no action lay for the infliction of emotional distress unless it was a foreseeable consequence of negligent physical harm.[12] The rule was an arbitrary one, but it served to reduce the number of such claims. Similarly, such claims were often dismissed because the loss suffered by the plaintiff was too uncertain. This was also an arbitrary barrier, since certainty barriers were waived for pain and suffering on a physical injury.[13]

Claims for damages for emotional distress are now commonplace, whether or not physical harm has resulted, and whether or not the claim sounds in tort or contract law. Tourists routinely sue their travel agents when booked in shoddy hotels, airlines are sued for near-misses, and Doris Barnett was awarded $400,000 for emotional trauma when she was told that she had not won the California lottery because her ball had popped out of the winning slot.[14]

Such claims are popular with law teachers, who note that emotional distress may be deeply felt, and that arbitrary barriers to recovery give plaintiffs less than full compensation for their harm.[15] From an economic perspective, such barriers may also be thought to result in inadequate incentives to take care. However, such claims might easily be fraudulent, with barriers to recovery eliminating wasteful litigation. In addition, restrictions on recovery for emotional distress usually promote the virtue of fortitude.

Fortitude both requires and reduces pain. One shows fortitude by carrying on without complaining in the face of pain or the prospect of suffering. Without pain there is no fortitude. But with fortitude the pain is lessened. The injured person suffers less himself, and passes on less of his pain to those around him. When the pain is great, he excites the admiration of those who know of his loss, and teaches them how to bear pain. By contrast, the whiner magnifies his own pain and passes it on to those near him.

The extent to which pain is felt is therefore a function of personal character, as well as of the circumstances which occasion pain. A state which inculcates fortitude through its legal regime may thus be a happier one than a state which smirks at fortitude and rewards the whiner.

Legal imperialism benefits lawyers: the decline of professional virtues

Lawyers have traditionally insisted on the need for strong professional virtues. In commending the study of law, Blackstone said that a lawyer should have an 'affectionate loyalty to the king, a zeal for liberty and the constitution, a sense of real honour, and well-grounded principles of religion'.[16] Making due allowance for differences in constitutional principles, the best lawyers I have known have always exhibited these virtues.

How did it come, then, that lawyers participated in the attack on social norms? Public choice theories suggest that concentrated groups with greater access to the levers of power will use their clout to transfer wealth to themselves from more dispersed groups.[17] As one such concentrated group, with special access to judges and legislators, lawyers might champion legal changes which expand their work and increase their fees.

Lawyers can therefore be expected to use their clout to expand the bounds of law by inventing new causes of action. Existing actions might also be muddied by the introduction of vague norms of 'fairness', since imprecise norms are more likely to be litigated than clear ones. Nor should one expect lawyers to promote attitudes of cheerful acceptance of harm and of forgiveness for one's tortfeasors.

Beyond this, legal and social sanctions compete, in the sense that stronger legal norms are needed when social sanctions fail to deter wrongful conduct. For this reason, the weakening of social norms through the expansion of legal remedies will benefit lawyers. In Hell, Grant Gilmore observed, there will be nothing but law.[18]

Lawyers mirror degraded contemporary social norms: liberal sentiments and appellate judges

There is, however, an alternative explanation for the expansion of the law. Like others in society, lawyers are affected by the decline in social sanctions. A lowering tide sinks all boats. The professional norms which constrained legal imperialism in the past are less strong today, and this has contributed to the litigation explosion.

To see this, one must understand the role of appellate courts in a legal system. If the losing party were never granted a right of appeal, then different trial courts in the same jurisdiction would develop their own bodies of law. Apart from ensuring uniformity, appellate courts also police trial judge misbehaviour. The trial judge who applies the law in a well-ordered legal system must attract less attention than the innovator who extends the law through the creation of novel remedies. The innovator will be applauded by the trial lawyers from whose ranks he rose, and from whom his future colleagues will be recruited. They will cite him more frequently in their legal briefs and law review articles, for his inventiveness offers them more business. In addition, the innovator, more ready than his colleagues to cut through legal barriers to advance broad political goals, can expect to be lionised by the press and by liberal interest groups. None of us is immune to flattery, and the innovator not infrequently comes to regard himself as wise and more caring than his more traditional colleagues.

In the 19th century, judicial misbehaviour of this type was policed by appellate courts, which reversed crowd-pleasing judgments on appeal. In this century, however, many appellate judges have come to share the liberal sentiments which they were appointed to monitor. Such judges—Douglas in America, Lord Denning in England, Laskin in Canada—became popular heroes, and often appeared immensely pleased at this. While their brethren have traditionally courted anonymity, the new breed of appellate judge sought recognition. Think, for example, of Lord Denning, who began a wrongful death judgement with 'It was bluebell time in Kent . . .,'[19] and who took pride in the law school T-shirts which bore his name.[20]

This change in judicial attitudes might plausibly be attributed to changes in social conventions, with appellate judges coming to share the values of an age of narcissism. In the past, a judge might have been satisfied to serve his profession in relative obscurity. Today, however, the sense of duty to one's profession, or to the law, is a good deal weaker, and the impulse to shine a great deal stronger. And if, in the process, one erases the line between law and politics, who is left to complain of judicial apostasy? In this way, modern societies get the law they deserve.

Conclusion

In the past, legal remedies reinforced social sanctions, through an added layer of penalties and through the instruction law offered on virtuous conduct. Today, however, law is more likely to undercut social norms. Legal norms are often inconsistent with social ones, particularly in the realm of family conduct. Truly wrongful behaviour is inadequately deterred by criminal penalties. Finally, social norms are weakened by the expansion of law, since a greater legal remedy excludes a weaker social one.

CHAPTER 3

Ridicule as a Means of Resisting Outlandish and Socially Damaging Ideas

Digby Anderson

The problem: why do modern societies treat outlandish ideas such as political correctness or the normalcy of single parenthood so seriously?

The son of an American university professor recently came home from school and was asked by his father what he had been taught that day. The teacher had, apparently, taught the class about the three great centres of civilisation, 'Athens, Rome, and Ghana'.

Future generations will look back on the 1990s in disbelief that educated people should take such ideas seriously. The notion that Ghana should be equated with Rome and Athens, and to the exclusion of Jerusalem, will appear to them *ridiculous*, that is, deserving of ridicule. Their question will be: why was late 20th century society incapable of laughing at patently ridiculous ideas?

Can a society lose the capacity or confidence to ridicule, and what are the consequences of such a loss?

In fact, the wilder inanities of political correctness are not the only ridiculous ideas to be treated seriously in present times, and the 1990s is not the first decade to accord intellectual respect and prolonged attention to ideas which should obviously be greeted with scorn, treated as 'beyond the pale' and 'laughed out of court'. For at least the last half century the civilized societies of the West have been faced with a series of outlandish ideas, some evil, some preposterous but harmless, some both evil and preposterous. And it is becoming clear that they are startlingly inept at handling them.

25

I am not here referring to ideas which are challenging, difficult, subversive, or dangerous, ideas such as Marxism and Freudianism. It may well be that these were granted too much respect and, in the case of Marxism, excessively prolonged and uncritical respect, but they were ideas with a serious intellectual content. It was right that they be respected and taken seriously.

Modern intellectuals may be drawn to ideas for unintellectual reasons. They have a number of conceits which such ideas flatter, not least that of putting the world to rights or at least tidying it up. It might have been better for humanity, especially that part of it that lived in the Soviet bloc, if intellectuals had not taken Marxism so seriously for so long, but there is nothing to be surprised about in their taking it seriously initially.

The outlandish ideas are quite a different case. Here we see the complex, sophisticated, mature, and successful society of Western Europe and North America confronted by ideas which are simplistic, naive, infantile, untried, and unworkable. And what has been its reaction? It has rolled over, given up, and let the nonsense walk all over it. In the 1960s, Anglo-American culture, steeped in the wisdom of thousands of years of sophisticated religion in the shapes of Judaism and Christianity, was asked to take seriously the mantras and peace moanings of Hippiedom. Within months, intellectual professors, worldly businessmen and robust truck drivers, respectable Midwestern parents and ministers of religion, not to mention national leaders, presidents, and prime ministers, not only genuflected to the inanity in the young but were sticking flowers in their own hair. It took no serious pressure at all to persuade the inheritors of the wisdom of Israel, Aristotle, Aquinas, and Newton to trample all over their priceless inheritance chanting silly slogans.

The outlandish ideas lead to social problems such as family collapse and crime: they are not just an intellectual problem

In the 1970s and 1980s, this same civilized society, built on the family, was asked to consider the ideas not just that homosexuals and voluntary lone-parent families might be tolerated, but that they be accorded as much value and social approval as the traditional family. And within a few years, what had been once regarded as unusual, deviant, unproductive, parasitical, or even perverted ways of life were taken into the mainstream of culture and affirmed as just another 'lifestyle', more, an equally valid way of life. Or consider the process whereby counselling, a practice almost entirely without tested scientific basis and evidence of cure, now sits in hospitals and surgeries alongside elaborately trialled pharmaceuticals and the most advanced surgery, posing and accepted as an equally important 'treatment'.

Some of the outlandish idealists probably hurt few people: an instance is the modern revival of vegetarianism, the people Orwell laughed at so loudly, ridiculing their fat bottoms and dismissing them as cranks. But even here, the wider phenomenon of healthism, that obsession with adding a few months to one's existence by a tortuous and tortured regime of diet, self-denial, and exercise, is far from harmless, especially when taken up by politicians and forced on those who would rather live 75 full years than 75 and a half narcissistically neurotic ones. The acceptance of homosexual practice as normal must be implicated in the death of many of those who have died in the AIDS carnage. The growth of the acceptance of single parenthood is closely entwined with the growth of single parenthood itself—one in three children in inner city areas is being brought up without a father. It is a phenomenon that damages children themselves and wider society, since it is linked to higher delinquency rates and lower educational attainment. Moreover, it is the taxpayer who is forced to take on the financial duties of the absent and irresponsible parent.

The singular and increasing inability of modern society to handle outlandish ideas appropriately is not then a problem only for intellectual life. It is linked with some of the most serious social problems of the age. Modern society has lost the confidence to dismiss outlandish ideas 'out of hand'. It has also lost the *art* of dismissing them. Part of that art is ridicule. If we can see why that confidence and art have been lost, we might see how they can be found again and the social problems the loss has caused may be reduced.

It should be re-emphasized that the peculiar prominence, even dominance of outlandish ideas today cannot be explained by the power of the ideas themselves or the strength of their adherents; in the early days at least, hippies, homosexuals, single parents, and political correctness fanatics were minorities, and minorities on the margins of society. Nor were their ideologies elaborate or powerful. They were, once, derided as outlandish. The answer to the puzzle must be sought in the response of mainstream society to these ideas and people. Why did civilized society, why did intellectuals, why did middle America and middle England roll over?

The key to the response to outlandish ideas: the worship of 'debate'

The way civilized society responded to outlandish ideas has two key features. The first is *debate*. Modern society, especially the modern intellectual, believes in the importance of debate. The intellectual almost worships it. It is true that the worship is not always sincere: the intellectual debate that led to a revival of market and conservative thinking in the 1970s was scarcely welcomed by the literati. But to talk of worship is not purely a colourful use of language. Recently in Britain, a Church of England priest wrote a book explaining that he did not believe in God. He did not believe in a God outside man, in his words, 'out there'. This man was preaching about the God in which he did not believe, consecrating bread and wine into the God in which he did not believe, reading to his parishioners the word of God in which he did not believe, and comforting dying parishioners about to pass to an afterlife in which he did not believe. Clearly an outlandish situation. His Bishop, the Bishop of Chichester, gave him a year to think about matters and when he still did not believe in God, fired him. Immediately 65 other priests wrote to the press attacking the decision to dismiss the priest. They thought the church ought to be wide enough to accommodate—and pay—priests who did not believe in God. Even more interesting, they protested because the affair had not been *debated.* They expressed no worries about God or disbelief in Him in their letter. What was the top of their priorities, their value system, their theology, was debate.

Debate is, then, a highly valued concept in Western civilized countries. It is true that ordinary people do not use debate to arrive at many of the judgements that inform their daily lives, and would think it pedantic to do so. But even they are forever being urged by more intellectual persons to test such daily habits by the measures of debate. Civilized people, it is said, do not just dismiss ideas or practices they find unusual, repellent, or ridiculous. They listen to their opponents' arguments for them, consider such arguments, test them, and pass a considered judgement on them. Individuals do this. Institutions, notably universities, are set up to encourage this. Governments do this. A free press is justified by its role in doing this. Ideas, as it were, are thought to have a *right* to be debated. If the idea is about behaviour, as in the case of homosexuality or single parenthood, then there is also a consensus about what the debate should try to establish. It should try to find out whether the idea and behaviour will lead to more good than harm. And what debaters look for in reaching such a judgement is evidence about how much good and harm is done, and to whom. So the way to treat, say, those advocating the rights of lesbian couples to adopt or have artificially inseminated children is to discuss the matter in an open and frank way, maybe commission research on what the outcomes of such arrangements have been, whether such children can be shown to have fared better or worse than others in terms of educational performance or social problems, then decide whether, on balance, the claim can be accepted or not.

In fact, the vetting procedure for new outlandish claims may not even go this far. Often the onus of proof is given to the society: if it cannot show that one-parent families, vegetarianism, or New Ageism does net *harm*, then it not only has no right to stop them, it has no right to treat them as less worthy than established social forms. They should be allowed centre stage as another way and given equal rights to established ideas when it comes to a TV debate or a Social Security handout. In some cases the process goes further. If they are now accepted and previously were not, then compensation may be due for the past stigmatising treatment. We should place more curricular emphasis on Ghana than Athens, give the lesbian couples more handouts than the married couples to make up for past repression.

Past societies had the good sense to put some ideas beyond debate and some behaviours beneath consideration

In fact we shall see that both assumptions—that debate is an unqualified good to which ideas have a right, and that its purpose should be to establish whether the idea or behaviour does more good than harm—are highly questionable and likely to lead to increasing social disruption and decay. It is not obvious that harmful consequences should be the only reason for denying a claim, nor that every outlandish idea is worthy of debate. If a consequentialist debate is the central defence of an orderly, civilized society, then that society will be left almost totally defenceless before any novelty.

Even more fundamentally, it is obvious that past societies, both primitive and civilized, have taken trouble to place certain matters beyond debate. All societies have their prohibitions. In modern societies these tend to be by 'rational' law and discretionary authority given to certain individuals and institutions. But even these societies have a few of the prohibitions that characterized primitive societies; prohibitions of custom for which no reasons are given, namely taboos. And earlier civilized societies such as Rome had positive injunctions which were treated as givens rather than discussed or thought about, such as duties to family or nation, the duties of *pietas*.

A really outlandish idea: the case of necrophilia

To see what can happen when no limits to debate are placed and society's defences left entirely to consequentialist discussion, let us take the example

29

of a really outlandish proposal and practice, necrophilia. Necrophilia means erotic attraction to corpses. Necrophilia is not exclusive or discriminatory with regard to the age, sex, race, or even species of the corpse. It could be a stranger or one's deceased mother, a sheep taken at random from an abattoir or a much-loved dead dog. Enough said to show the idea and behaviour are certainly outlandish. What we might call 'active' necrophilia is, if this be the right term, making love to corpses. Activ*ist* necrophilia is the intellectual and political movement to win a place for necrophilia as equal to other forms of sexual behaviour and to achieve the rights of necrophiliacs to satisfy their desires and to be undiscriminated against for so doing.

How would modern society respond to the claims of the necrophiliac activist? On past form, after some time ignoring him, someone would give him a hearing. After all, it may sound outlandish but then haven't all sorts of ideas and behaviour been dismissed as outlandish, which are now accepted by everyone? And again, if we are going to persecute every outlandish idea simply because it's outlandish, we are going to have a very repressive state. At least initially, all the activist is asking for is for him, his friends, and their dead friends to be left in peace. Haven't the police better things to do than persecute people for their sexual feelings? The key question surely is whether the necrophiliacs are doing harm to anyone else. If not, let them be. It may be bizarre behaviour, but it should not be criminal.

Classical liberalism, psychoanalysis, public health, and consequentialism cannot find anything wrong with necrophilia

Partly to establish whether it does harm anyone else, partly because we should know before we condemn, partly because it might be interesting, partly because the activist, like anyone else, has a right to be heard, a debate is accorded. Such a debate would be unlikely, in the case of necrophilia, to convert the civilized society *en masse* to active necrophilia, but there are strong grounds for thinking that once the right to debate was conceded, necrophilia would win toleration. The Campaign for Necrophiliac Rights (CNR) would do well to lead off their case with a philosopher. He could easily show that necrophilia hurts 'no-one' in the accepted sense of that word: indeed not a single complaint has ever been made by the object of the necrophiliac's attentions. No danger is threatened to minors. And the matter is essentially a private affair. Much quoting of J. S. Mill might take place; though it would pass over even this champion of debate's remark in his essay on Coleridge, that there must, in any society, be something settled and not called into question, some protected belief. The overall conclusion would be that the practice gives happiness to the necrophiliac and neither harms nor disturbs anyone else.

A classical-liberal economist could easily be found to discuss whether the practice imposed costs on others and he would talk about externalities, private and public goods, and Pareto optimality. Though the language would be different from the philosopher's, the argument would be essentially the same, as would the conclusion. A psychoanalyst would testify that necrophiliacs were more likely to do harm to others if their desires were repressed than if they were satisfied. Public health officials would find no threat to public health provided certain safe sex practices and hygiene procedures were followed. Medical ethicists would explain that there was no overriding need for consent forms but, in the light of their experience with euthanasia, they could design one if necessary. The necrophiliac activists themselves would sieve through history to find great men and women, religious leaders, generals, kings, and saints who were necrophiliacs, or would have been had they not lived in societies irrationally prejudiced against it. They would show that necrophiliacs were ordinary men and women, decent people who held down jobs, brought up children, fought for their country, and paid their taxes. Their surveys would show that at one time or another, 27 per cent of the American population had had or fantasized a necrophiliac episode.

There would be opposition, especially from non-intellectuals. Midwesterners, provincial people, rednecks would find the whole idea disgusting. For a time they would seem on the verge of defeating the idea. Then the press would discover that the leader of the Campaign for Decent America had links with unsavoury, discriminatory causes and he would be discredited. Lingering doubts among the intellectuals would be finally dispelled when a prominent artist/novelist/playwright/sculptor would explain that the denial of necrophiliac freedom was a denial of artistic freedom.

How societies used to dismiss outlandish ideas: restoring the capacity to ridicule

The point is simple: once the right to debate is conceded and the purpose of the debate accepted, the case is lost. Previous societies, no less civilized than this one, knew this. They knew necrophilia was disgusting, obviously disgusting. They knew it was both perverted and a violation of something sacred. For them, evidenced harm was not the only measure of evil. In another example also involving death, it is wrong to break a promise to one's mother even after she has died and cannot be hurt by the betrayal. It is wrong to fail to keep a will. Obligations to parents, alive or dead, were not terminable or negotiable. Former socieites would have dismissed pleas for a debate about such matters with ridicule.

These societies believed in debate too. They were happy to debate as between Protestantism and Catholicism, socialism and the market. But that did not mean they would debate anything. In such societies, in nearly all societies except this one, there were ideas and behaviour viewed as so perverted, evil, or bizarre, that the civilized response, far from being discussion, was instant dismissal, contempt, laughter, a shrug of the shoulder, ridicule.

It is of the essence of dismissal and ridicule that those who practice them, successfully, do not give elaborate reasons for them. They are justified not by debate but by the mutual sympathies of those who engage in them, those appealed to who stand by, and even by those whom they were done to. But we can go some way to sketch the framework in which they occur. Such a framework is anything but simplistic. First, such a society was not too worried about dismissing new ideas because it knew that dismissing an idea is not the worst thing one can do to it. James Fitzjames Stephen puts the point well, commenting on the ballad:

> Cursed be the coward that ever he was born
> Who did not draw the sword before he blew the horn.

Having to fight for a hearing of one's idea tests it. Dismissal does not kill a good idea, it strengthens it: until a man 'has formed opinions . . . for which he is prepared to fight, there is no hardship in his being compelled by social intolerance to keep them to himself and to those who sympathise with him'.[1]

Keeping deviant ideas in the shadows

Such societies had a sophisticated shading of ideas and behaviour in which some were mainstream, some beyond the pale, and yet others in the shadows. It is not a simple matter of ideas and behaviour being accepted or rejected, as is so often argued. Being silenced is an elastic sort of experience. When Oscar Wilde's friend, Lord Alfred Douglas, wrote of the love that dare not speak its name, the phrase suggests a great injustice. In fact, Douglas and, even more, Wilde himself spent much of their lives talking about nothing else than this love and indulging in it. In poem and conversation, in manner and in photograph, Wilde positively flaunted the love that Douglas would have us believe was speechless. What Wilde and Douglas wanted was not to be left alone to talk about and indulge in this love. If any-thing approached hell for either of them it was precisely being left alone. Even Wilde's flaunting did not go far enough to satisfy Douglas. André Gide recalls talking with them in North Africa. Amidst a continuous din about the unspeakable love, he tells the tale of Wilde and Douglas meeting at the Savoy and Douglas crying, 'I want everyone in the restaurant to see us; I want everyone to say, "There goes Oscar Wilde and his minion" '.[2]

The sophisticated society is not prepared to treat all ideas and behaviour equally. It has its mountain tops, its plains, its backwaters, and its caves. And it allocates this idea to this place and that to that. It is aware that granting debate on the plain in full public gaze immediately grants legitimacy of a sort and will start a process difficult to arrest. It will keep the mountain tops for the proclamation of public doctrine, ideas, and behaviour hallowed by consensus and time. And there is a fine process by which the idea of the cave and the shadows can, if it is good, reach the plain. But it has to show that it has resemblances, values it shares, with the established ideas, and it has to serve its apprenticeship in the shadows.

Society not a set of ideas to be debated but a set of habits to be proved in practice over time

The sophisticated society knows that ideas can be judged by more than whether they are true or not, and behaviour by more than whether it results in measurable good or harm. Even truths uttered in the wrong place may be spiteful, hurtful, or offensive, and the old society had a deep comprehension of offensiveness. There are acts which hurt not someone else's goods or physical freedom, but their honour, their family's honour, acts which offend against human decency. Even modern societies have a small domain of the sacred which is a no-go area for public debate as distinct from private conversation. But they have lost the old understanding, the down-to-earth understanding that endless debate is not the most important thing in life, that with societies, as with individuals, there has to be an end to the talking for there is work to be done and a life together to be lived under shared assumptions. Debate can educate a society, but it can also paralyse it. Moreover, if all is debatable and if all claims to debate and indulgence are to be taken seriously, then any sense of priority and order will be lost. If all is debate-worthy, nothing is. As Plato understood with democracy, so with debate; if it is pushed too far it ends in chaos and repression.

Whether ideas can be shown to cause harm is not the only reason for dismissing them

The traditional understanding was also that the fact that no harm could be demonstrated to date in some new behaviour did not mean that harm might not result in the future. More, harm was not the only criterion. These societies believed in the difference between normal and abnormal, right and wrong, respectable and unrespectable. They knew the real test of ideas and behaviour was what they did to the perpetrator, not others. And they had a sense too of the frivolous. American courts still have the power to throw out claims on the grounds not only that they are unfounded, but are frivolous. They would clog up the courts if allowed. If modern society loses that sense and allows all claims, all entrants to debate, it will clog its morality, its culture, its very civilization.

I have said that these senses of the old society were not explicit justifications for ridiculing outlandish ideas, but the framework which made possible the distinction between mainstream and outlandish ideas. Just as they were rarely explicit, so they resist summary. But I suppose many of them would be regarded today as *prejudices* and that is something many of them share. The word would be pejorative today, of course. But that is no reason to reject it. Prejudices can be wrong and evil. But many are neither wrong nor evil. Indeed, if prejudice is short-cut thinking, a fine sensibility which can measure the worth of an innovation without making explicit or even knowing the exact grounds for its speedy judgement, then it may be something no society can do without.

The necessity of prejudice: of being able to dismiss 'out of hand' or with laughter

The old society was not embarrassed or worried by prejudice. It was happy with it. It was mature and comfortable—sometimes too comfortable—in its varied topography, its subtle hierarchy, its inherited priorities. It understood itself as a society, a set of values and practices, not as an intellectual proposition continually liable to be called out by some new contending idea. The recognition or at least acceptance and use of prejudice is society's key defence against barbarism. Without the subtleties of prejudice, society is left without a sense of proportion and shading, and is hence prey to destructive ideas and behaviours, to necrophilia and its legion cousins which consequentialist intellectual arguments can never resist. Worse, without these prejudices and a sense of proportion, there is no sense of humour. The root of ridiculous in Latin is in laughter. Without the prejudices there is no laughter, nothing to make mouths open in shock, eyebrows raise in amusement, or gazes turn down in scorn. Imagine a society of faces that did no such things, the society in which ridicule is banished. And lest it be supposed that no one would be so stupid as to try and control a society's facial expressions, there is another incident from an American university. It had been reported that some faculty were not making eye contact with lady students and this was demeaning to the ladies. Faculty were to make eye contact with all students. On the other hand, they were not to keep eye contact with lady students too long. If they found it difficult to gauge the exact, politically correct duration for the maintenance of eye contact, they could attend special courses to learn.[3]

CHAPTER 4

Administering Punishment Morally, Publicly, and Without Excuse

Graeme Newman

Today's penologists totally confused as to what to do to criminals

Each generation tends, perhaps, to view its own age as that of crisis. So it is with some temerity that I offer the observation that the state of morality in advanced Western society, as the 20th century draws to a close, is deep in crisis, perhaps so deep that there may be no salvation. I am most uncomfortable in advancing this thesis, because it sounds as though I have become an old fogey, resentful of the young and their ideas, rigid in my beliefs, pathetically yearning for a return to the 'good old days'. But I am moved to take this position, especially in regard to punishment, because I think that the seriousness of the situation demands it.

The absolute confusion among academics and practitioners in the field of penology as to 'what to do' with those who have committed crimes is abundantly clear. When 'treatment' (in whatever guise) was abandoned in the 1970s as the solution to punishment, a void remained. In fact, no new solutions to punishment have emerged since prison became the panacea early in the 20th century.

Old punishments—branding, flogging, scolding, exile—all dismissed in favour of prison

Instead, the range of punishments has progressively been reduced. A cursory look at the range of punishments available up until the end of the 18th century is sufficient to demonstrate this: a wide variety of corporal punishments was available, many different kinds of social and cultural stigma and shame were routinely administered (e.g., branding); many public and communal punishments were considered appropriate (e.g., the pillory); and there were far more punishments that responded directly to the specific offence (e.g., the scold's bridle). Standard penology or 'corrections' text-books categorically reject these punishments of olden days as 'primitive'. They proclaim the emergence of prison as the wholesale response to serious crimes as 'progress'.

Yet this 'progress' has not brought with it any semblance of a solution to the problem of punishment. In the United States and other Western democracies, the numbers put in prison have increased dramatically in the last two decades. In the U.S. there were, in 1994, over one million people locked up. This would not be so bad if there were some moral reasoning that provided the justification for the wholesale use of this single punishment. But there is no attempt at moral justification for prison, except to assert that the practices of 200 years ago were 'primitive' or 'barbaric'.

Today's punishment not based on any moral justification

Treatment (or rehabilitation, depending on one's terminology) once provided the moral structure for punishment in the 20th century. But now it has gone and has been replaced by nothing else. How can such a drastic and destructive punishment as prison be justified on the basis of a negative philosophy that 'nothing works'? Why has no moral justification been developed for its wide-scale application? I emphasise *moral* here, because I am well aware that the major justification for prison use today is incapacitation and, less often, deterrence. These justifications are, however, political justifications, rather than moral justifications, because they are concerned essentially with order. Although it is reasonable and persuasive to argue that morality (and its political counterpart, justice) are impossible without order, I would also argue that order established without due concern for morality runs the risk of producing a society and culture of brutality and oppression. One needs morality as a protection against political domination, just as much as one needs a political order to boost and maintain morality.

Morality undermined by science and socialism

However, I have jumped ahead of myself. Let us return to the start: that we are in a state of crisis, this crisis is essentially a moral crisis, and that this crisis in morality is what lies at the heart of the problem of punishment today. What, precisely, is this moral crisis? I certainly do not claim to be the sole or even first discoverer of this crisis. It has been identified by many commentators, some religious, some educators, others social critics. I think, however, that Bloom's argument in his provocative book, *The Closing of the*

American Mind, is the most cogent: that the morality of the age has been undermined by a variety of ideologies, primarily those of neo-Marxists who gave up on morality, and embraced wholesale the Nietzschean philosophy of moral destruction.

I would not want to blame Nietzsche or even Marx for this course of events. The history of ideas in the 19th and 20th century is far more complicated than this. These great thinkers would not have had the actual social influence they have had on 20th century thought, morality, and politics, had not another revolution occurred virtually at the same time. I refer, of course, to the 'scientific revolution'—the seemingly necessary outcome of the industrial revolution. I think that the wholesale transmigration of science into the social thought of the 20th century has been far more effective in undermining the morality of the age than any other single factor. This requires some explanation.

In his famous essay, 'The Two Cultures', delivered in 1959, C. P. Snow lamented that the two spheres of knowledge or human understanding, the scientific and the literary, had developed apart, with the result that each was ignorant of the other. His essay sparked a huge debate around the world over specialisation in education, not to mention the relationship between culture and knowledge. Yet a curious omission in his essay (and continued in his later reply to his critics) was a discussion of how a blending of the two—science and literature—might affect the growth and development of morality and ethics. This omission appears even more curious when one takes into account Snow's other writings, which were based on a clear and uncompromising set of Christian principles. And here, I think, is the solution to the puzzle. Snow wrote his essay taking for granted a commonly shared set of Christian principles. In other words, he took morality for granted. So also did the scientists of his time. It was not until reflections concerning the development of the atom bomb, for example, that scientists began to realise that what they did necessarily involved moral assumptions of enormous magnitude. Einstein himself had recognised this, but its importance did not seep into the culture of scientists until much later. There seemed to be an assumption that, because the industrial revolution had produced so much that was beneficial to mankind—wealth, health, the conquering of space—that the scientific enterprise needed little moral justification.

In his response to critics, Snow admitted one fault: he had failed to give sufficient credence to social historians who, he agreed, had quite a lot to say about the condition of humankind, and who had worked scientifically to study the effects of, for example, the industrial revolution on ordinary people. Yet he overlooked in his essay and response to critics one crucial coming together of science and literature: that of the social sciences in general.

What science did to morality as social science

For if there were any significant event in the scientific revolution that could be identified in the history of science of the 20th century, it would surely be the application of scientific methods to the study of individuals and groups. That is, the growth and emergence of social science. My guess is that the rate of growth of the social sciences as fields of study, and the rate of growth as a field of employment in applied social science such as the field of human services—welfare, health care, personnel management, education, to name but a few—has far outstripped the rate of growth in the natural sciences.

And this, I suggest, is the problem. In this century there have been two powerful ideological forces at work: science and socialism. We should admit that the 19th century was the age of capitalism, a grand age that has passed. Left wing commentators have noted with pleasure that post-industrial society has now become post-modern society. Whatever we call it, we have to admit that socialism has been the moving spirit of the 20th century. And its age is also about to pass, if indeed it has not already passed. These two great forces, science and socialism, have worked together to produce the crisis of our age which Bloom and others have lamented: the loss of morality.

While it would take many pages to describe the process of the dissolution of moral thought in the 20th century, I should like to offer two main reasons for this loss. The first relates directly to science, the second to socialism.

Science stands for the destruction of value. Its rules of method are rigid of necessity. While modern scientists now understand that there are values and ethics involved in what they do, these are seen as secondary to the main objectives of science; to understand and control the natural world. Scientists assume the right to investigate any phenomenon simply because it is there. What happens to the results of their endeavours is a matter for society to decide, and is essentially society's responsibility. That is, what scientists do must remain and be seen as amoral: it is this devotion to 'objectivity' (or pursuit of it) that lies at the very heart of scientific method. Without it, the entire edifice of science would collapse.

It is possible to read the history of science as one that demonstrates that major progress in science has resulted from a process different from the objective scientific method as has mostly been assumed. But a close reading of such historians of science will show that they are talking more about power, politics, and competition among *scientists*, rather than competing *values*. Kuhn, for example, in his provocative *The Structure of Scientific Revolutions*, while showing that 'discoveries' have resulted from anything but a rational progression of research and thought, nevertheless clearly argues that without the traditional scientific method, the process of science would collapse, and the discoveries along with it.

Science teaches probability and uncertainty not least about who is good and bad

As science has progressed, not only has it refused to consider value as an integral part of science, but it has advanced the notion of probability as a keystone of scientific research design and essentially as a mode of explanation. That is, the modern view of science is one that is built on uncertainty. In the classroom I have, on more than one occasion, advocated the necessity for scholars and social scientists to learn to live with uncertainty, to view it as the necessary outcome of a scientific or rational view of life. We know that in order to get through each day, each of us must behave 'as if' certainty prevailed, as if the basic things of life—time, space, order—were entirely predictable. It is uncertainty that my students find extremely difficult either to understand or accept: particularly those students who come to class wearing insignia that suggest the very opposite orientation to life, such as those who wear crosses round their necks, or other religious insignia. For it is in the sphere of religion, of course, where uncertainty is banished. The great religious philosophers of the 19th century, such as Kierkegaard, and much earlier, such as Luther, devoted much of their time to trying to deal with uncertainty: that is, the necessity of (and difficulty in maintaining) 'faith'. I am most ambivalent about having promoted the loss of faith in my classroom. But I cannot see how I could avoid it if I wanted to teach also the modern view of science. In my opinion, the implications are considerable for penology and other applied social sciences.

A psychotherapist I know recently complained to me: 'It seems that the more psychology I learn, the less certain I am in dealing with my clients' problems'. Read the texts and research of criminology and penology. The distinctions in character, for example, between those who are in prison and the rest of us have been steadily eroded by social science. Convicts have no distinguishing features, we are told, except for the fact that 'they' are in prison. It is criminals who have, by their behaviour, identified themselves.

From here, it is a small step to socialism.

Socialism: equality applied to individuals, groups, and cultures

Socialism is perhaps not an accurate word to describe the ethos or 'culture' that has emerged in the 20th century to destroy value. Bloom argues that the neo-Marxists embraced Nietzsche, producing a 'Nietzscheanisation of the left', as he called it (an appropriately ugly expression). But Nietzsche argued for the eradication of value by raw superhuman power, an ethic that can hardly be said to fit with the basic ethic of Marxism: that of equality, especially the eradication of power relations and the exploitation of man by man. Why did Marxists incorporate a philosophy so foreign to their basic principles? A simple answer: in order to justify their impatience to take power, rather than waiting, as Marx advocated, for the revolution to emerge. But there is a more profound reason.

The problem of the destruction of value among the left socialist ideologies is internal to their ideology itself. As Marx would say, their ethic bears the seeds of its own destruction. I refer to the prime value of socialist and Marxist thought: equality. This ideal has bound the many ideologies of the left together for most of this century. And while it has remained an ideal, it has been a powerful value. But in the latter part of the 20th century it has ceased to be an ideal, and rather is used as a means of defining everyday relations among individuals and groups. And it is here that it has foundered, and produced unhappiness and human conflict. Let me explain.

Equality is a slippery, difficult word. I do not want to enter into the many debates over its meaning: such as those over Marx's famous 'each according to his needs' expression. Rather, I want to look at the relationship of socialist ideology to the social sciences: for it is here, particularly in Europe, and more specifically in the United Kingdom, that socialism as an ethic has found a comfortable home. While equality is used as an ethic and ideal to defend the downtrodden and poor against the excesses of the privileged, I have no difficulty in accepting, and indeed lauding the concept. But in these times, the concept of equality has been applied to the practical relations among individuals and groups, and this application has issued directly from the work in the social sciences: that work itself issuing directly from the natural scientific ethic of objectivity and amorality: the idea of moral relativism, or more precisely, the approach to cultures established and promoted by the anthropologists of the 1950s and 1960s: cultural relativism. The argument runs something like this: equality is the supreme value, therefore all people should be made equal, and all cultures and human groups are of equal value. But here is the contradiction: since equality is the supremely good value, any culture or society that allows or promotes inequality is evil.

However, since all cultures are of equal value, no culture can be said to be evil. The ethic or value of equality therefore collapses under the weight of its own contradiction. While contradictions in the abstract can endure, and perhaps should, when they are applied in practice they lead inevitably to conflict and dissolution.

The applied example of the equality principle is that of the current fad for 'diversity' and in some places, the attempt, using 'affirmative action' to 'correct' the imbalances of inequality. Taken further and applied to education, for example, this means that we should make sure all our children receive an education in equal parts of all cultures, valuing not one over the other. This is, of course, a sheer impossibility, and also denies the real differences among cultures, differences that are often vast and unbridgeable.

Equality: the murderer no different from you and me

Lest it seem that I have strayed from the topic of punishment, let me hasten to add that I have reached the exact point of intersection of the moral crisis of our times with that of punishment. For it must be patently clear that one cannot morally justify punishing another if one takes the position that the other is one's equal in concrete moral terms. Taken to its extreme (though this is not an extreme but standard view in academic criminology): the murderer is no different from you or me. Because one cannot pass moral judgements on one's fellow being without imposing one's own moral standard, and since all moral standards (cultures) are of equal value, who is to say that what the murderer did was wrong and therefore deserving of punishment? We see this logic most clearly in the popular argument used against the death penalty: that the death penalty is simply State-condoned murder. Here we have the familiar destruction of value by the application of the 'ethic' of equality: the murderer is raised to a level equal to the State (or vice versa). The central crisis of morality in this age is well exposed by this example. The question of punishment has been reduced to one of power relations, to a political question, and has avoided completely the moral question of: is it right to intentionally kill another human being for either no reason or a selfish reason (the murderer) or for an historically legislated reason (the State)?

The crisis in morality contains serious implications both for the philosophy of punishment, and for the practical aspects of punishment policy in criminal justice. This is because the two schools of punishment justification—the retributive and the utilitarian—bear an uncanny resemblance to the two cultures problem that has produced the levelling of val-

45

ues. While much has been said for and against these two schools of thought, a brief summary of their supposed differences helps to clarify how, perhaps, they have arisen quite in conjunction with the conditions of moral relativism that have emerged in the 20th century.

Retributive views of punishment

Let us consider the typical retributive view, which is essentially one which argues that individuals who break the laws of a country deserve to be punished. Such individuals are imbued with choice and rationality. The laws may be good or bad, just or unjust, but offenders choose to break them, and by so doing, choose to be punished. Essentially, the retributive position is as simple as this. There are many (I among them) who have identified finer distinctions of retributive theory. But when it's all boiled down, it is the pristine simplicity of the justification that is its strength: if you make a choice, you reap (for good or ill) the consequences. This is the concept of individual freedom and responsibility at its simplest and its best. It is an ethic of individual responsibility.

Utilitarian views of punishment

Compare the utilitarian position. We begin with something that looks like a value statement about all individuals in society, the elementary form of the equality principle: the greatest good for the greatest number (espoused in various forms by Bentham, Beccaria, Rousseau, Pascal, and many others of the 18th century Enlightenment). Everything issues from this principle. Individuals and groups are punished for the good of society, not for their own good. But one can see that punishing (i.e., the intentional infliction of pain and suffering) individuals on behalf of the greater good goes against the ethic of equality: for how can we treat those as equals whom we are at the same time subjecting to a process of suffering which requires that they be the subjects of domination (punishment)? The utilitarian view of punishment is political: it raises the State to a level above individuals, arguing that individuals are not and should not be equal to the State. Thus, the simplest and clearest statement of the utilitarian justification of punishment is that punishment is essentially a political act, and justifiable on those terms. The State is above the individual, and thus need not concern itself with the ethic of equality. This logic has led to the contradictions that have occurred in many Marxist states: a dictatorship arises, in which individuals have few rights at all: they are equal all right, equally oppressed and denied.

46

The utilitarian position has essentially two intellectual roots, both of which blossomed in the Enlightenment of the 18th century. The first was the attempt to apply a systematic, scientific approach to solving the problems of society. If we take Bentham as the supreme example in the area of criminal punishment, we see that he declared himself the enemy of values, especially those embodied in the criminal law. If he did affirm a value, it was that of self-interest or pleasure, since he declared all pain as evil, and all pleasure as good, thus laying the foundations for the 'ethic' of narcissism that has dominated the latter half of the 20th century in the West. Bentham applied as best he could a 'scientific' approach to the problems of how to organise a society, and how to motivate and control individual behaviour. His was a systematic reduction of human and social problems to rules of logic (granting his premises), and sometimes arithmetical calculations (though this criticism of him has been overstated).

Secondly, the majority of the utilitarians saw it as their mission to fight oppression in one way or another. Since they worked on the basic premise of the greatest good for the greatest number, they jumped to the conclusion that because criminals tended to come from the poorer classes, they were criminal because they were poor, not because they chose to be criminal. Thus, it followed that it was not morally correct to punish individuals who did not choose to commit a crime, and worse, if what they had done was destructive of society, then it was necessary to 'correct' the criminals rather than punish them. Thus arose the devious and highly effective 'medical model'—the ethos of rehabilitation, and the transformation of punishment into 'corrections', all the time under the guise that it was somehow more morally correct to treat criminals as though they were sick, than it was to punish them.

Rehabilitation

The era of rehabilitation represented a wholesale incursion of the scientific revolution into penology, particularly the deterministic view of science as applied to human action. According to this view, no individual's actions were consciously chosen: they were the result of causal factors that stretched way beyond the individual (whether biological, unconscious, sociological or so on). And when the canons of science were finally applied to assess whether in fact the new scientific methods of rehabilitation 'worked', the plaintive conclusion in the 1970s was: 'nothing works'. By this time, the dominance of the uncertainty principle in the natural sciences had caught up with the social sciences. Such a conclusion was only to be expected. The shallowness of the rehabilitative or medical model was thus revealed and a moral void remained. Corrections officials and administrators have no moral philosophy to guide them. They, as well as their inmates, bear the burden of society's irresponsible morality (if that is what it is): 'lock 'em up and throw away the key'.

I used the expression 'morally correct'. This demonstrates how moral choice and values have been transformed into questions of politics: since today's popular terminology refers to 'values' that are 'politically correct'. There is no attempt even to hide the fact that the 'value' is purely political and of little moral consequence.

I suggest that the question of moral responsibility for doing wrong (however defined), and for responding to that wrong with a deserved punishment, has little to do with whether one is rich or poor, happy or sad, oppressor or oppressed. Rather, it must be related to the extent to which individuals and societies are held responsible for their actions. If this responsibility is vacated, either by individuals, or by entire societies—then we have a crisis.

Visibility and punishment

Western society has vacated its responsibility for punishing criminals by its massive use of prison, a punishment so uncontrollable, so isolated from society, that it serves well to allow society to forget about the criminals it punishes. A parent, if she smacks a child, takes full responsibility for that punishment: she lives with the consequences of that punishment and so does the child. But we in society do not have to live with the consequences of the punishment of prison, since individuals remain hidden away. It is a secretive, isolating punishment, one for which we do not have to take responsibility. Who could argue otherwise, when we see society's demand to lock up more and more people, but at the same time, its refusal to approve the expenditure of more money to build and staff more prisons?

And this brings me back to my original point: punishment policy in the field of criminal justice has been denuded of its morality. It has been reduced to a crass act of political domination, either in the service of deterrence, or in the service of the 'protection of society'. While one can make separate arguments as to the applicability and appropriateness of punishments for particular criminals using these justifications, they should not be allowed to dominate the moral sphere of punishment. They are not moral justifications, they are political. And, while their importance in maintaining a semblance of order may be considerable, we should not fool ourselves that order—especially a moral order—issues from a punishment system that is void of moral principles. More likely it is (and will be) the reverse: the more punishment is used in the name of deterrence, the more resentment is built up, and the less justifiable will the punishment appear to be, even political-ly. In a society which is devoid of value (i.e., one that has lost its culture), there is nothing to hold it together. It may be artificially held together for a while using strong deterrent punishment, but it cannot last.

Full and public moral punishment

In sum, we need to affirm clearly the right and responsibility of society to punish individuals who have broken the law. We should not allow ourselves the excuses that social science, conditioned by the moral relativism of sci-ence and the socialist ideology of equality, has proffered us: that those who break the law did so not of their own choosing, but because they were sick or poor or oppressed. We need to reject the demoralised view of social sci-ence, and insist that individuals take full responsibility for their actions, that no excuses are allowed, that criminals recognise that in a moral society, one of necessity reaps the benefits of one's choices. Make no mistake: the moral challenge rests squarely on both the criminals and society. Society must cease to hide behind prison as *the* solution to punishment. It must move as much punishment as possible out of the closet of prisons and into the open: punishments should be administered directly, openly, publicly, and without apology. They should convey a clear sense that this is the right thing to do; that criminals deserve their punishment; that we undermine their moral character by denying them punishment, or at least by administering pun-ishment carried by a half-hearted attempt at rehabilitation.

I should add that I am not advocating a 'get tough' policy on criminals. The disgusting state of overcrowded prisons already applies such a policy. Rather, I am advocating a 'get moral' policy. Administer punishment responsibly. Demand of criminals that they recognise the morality of their behaviour, essentially that they recognise that they, and they alone (not soci-ety, their genes, or abusive fathers) are responsible for their crimes. And it is they, and they alone, who can repair the moral damage they have done by taking full responsibility for their actions, and accepting the punishment that is their due. The reader may be left to judge which punishments might fit such criteria. It will certainly mean revisiting and perhaps up-dating penalties once discarded as barbaric.

CHAPTER 5

Uniformity, Uniforms, and the Maintenance of Adult Authority

Douglas J. Den Uyl

Dress codes in government-funded schools: common till the 1960s

There was a time when public-school children in the United States were held to some kind of dress code. During the mid to late 1960s, for example, boys could not wear sideburns below the earlobes, blue jeans were forbidden (as were T-shirts), and hair had to be trimmed so that it did not hang over the ears. And although they were not forbidden, tennis shoes were frowned upon by the school administration as being a sign of slovenly dress. These specific requirements varied throughout the U.S. at the time. Almost everyone I have spoken to from that period, however, recalls being subjected to some sort of dress code.

The point, of course, is not so much what the exact requirements were, but rather that there *were* requirements and that they were being administered by a *public* school. It is difficult to imagine such requirements being instituted today, let alone proposed. Indeed, such proposals may at first seem a bit ludicrous in the wake of teenage pregnancy, guns in the schools, assaults on teachers, illiterate education performances, and general social breakdown. With all these problems dress codes might seem quaintly anachronistic.

Let me propose, nevertheless, that *all public-school children, especially in the upper grades, be made to wear uniforms during school hours.* There is no pretence being made here that this sort of proposal will cure the ills of the public school system, but perhaps if we explore what can be said in defence of such a proposal, some sort of cure can begin.[1]

Uniforms: not only practical advantages but a way adult society orders juvenile society

The most obvious and immediate benefit is cost. Although uniforms might require a slightly greater initial outlay than jeans and a T-shirt, the cost is likely to be borne only once in a school year. And since there are no fashions to keep up with, the parent is not confronted with having to maintain a wardrobe, even if the particular items in that wardrobe would be relatively inexpensive. Of course, it is also true that a single jeans (especially if they are designer jeans) and T-shirt ensemble can easily be *more* expensive than uniforms.

Cost, however, is only part of the benefit. Parents will be free from arguing with their children concerning the appropriateness of their dress. Standards of appropriateness are societal by nature. Yet without uniforms the 'society' that governs those standards would be that of the children. With uniforms, the adult world predominates. Fashions among children are not thereby obliterated; they are, however, relegated to those activities that are specifically oriented to the child or adolescent (e.g., play or dating). School is, or should be, the institutional means by which children are brought to adulthood. It is only fitting, therefore, that the standards of the adult world take preeminence there.

Uniforms distinguish children from adults: maintaining adult leadership

Uniforms have another function: they clearly distinguish the children from the adults. One immediate practical benefit of this is that those who may be 'hanging around' the schools and yet who are not themselves students (drug dealers, dropouts, child molesters) would be easily identified. Within the schools, the commonality of casual dress today, and the blending of appearances among the ages (younger looking older and older looking younger), makes it difficult to distinguish the students from the teachers. This has the effect, at least symbolically, of subordinating the adult to the child, because younger dress codes are the ones that tend to prevail.

But so what if children look a little older and we adults ostensibly age more slowly? Is it not desirable that we 'get along better' with the younger generation, and is not having more in common a significant factor in accomplishing that end? One clear cost in succumbing fully to this line of reasoning is the weakening of adult authority generally. Without supposing that the wearing of uniforms will reinstitute that authority on its own, the symbolism of uniforms is nevertheless a constant reminder of which world governs. And while many factors certainly contribute to the loss of authority these days, it seems absurd to pass up a relatively costless form of visible support.

Yet what seems just as critical as the issue of authority is the implication for the nature of role-modelling itself. It is simply not the case that being a 'buddy' to one's children or one's students is a desirable quality. What children want and need from adults is not additional companionship but leadership in the movement toward adulthood itself. Children by nature wish to become mature, but when the distinction between adults and children is hazed over or obliterated completely, guidance is missing and the message is that adults have nothing to contribute to the child's maturity. The child's own desires then come to be regarded as an adequate guide.[2]

Adults also wear uniforms at work as a sign of seriousness: uniforms say 'we are here to work not play'

It is precisely here that one may wish to counter with the argument that treating children more as adults by giving them more choices will better help them to mature than does labelling them as children (with uniforms). But this argument misses a significant feature of adult dress. The adult professional world is a world where conformity of dress and appropriate appearance predominate. While diversity exists, a certain conformity is part of all professional attire. That conformity is a way of signifying that one has come to the work environment with a serious intent. Attention can afterwards be directed to the important matters of the day. Uniforms for children would make a similar statement in a school context. They would say, in other words, that the children have come for the business of school, not play. Finally, it is not choice *per se* that matters, but intelligent choice. Putting dress in intelligent perspective is what uniforms are likely to inculcate as an attitude, much as professional dress does in the adult world.

It may, on the other hand, be tempting to take the opposite tack to the preceding argument. If the adult world is so conformist, uniforms should be opposed because this is the only time in their lives that children will have the freedom to be children. This sort of argument, however, is subject to rebuttals similar to those previously given. Part of being a child is learning how to be an adult. This argument 'let children be children' cannot be absolute or we would have to abandon our responsibilities as adults toward them. But since we have such responsibilities, each plea for a special dispensation has to be examined on its own merits. Abandoning uniforms does not deserve any special consideration on these grounds (as, for example, shielding children as long as possible from exposure to sexuality might), because, as noted above, schools are inherently adult-orienting institutions.

Uniforms can thus be of benefit in both concrete practical ways and in more indirect and symbolic ways. What is most beneficial generally is that the relationship between adults and children be one that accords with the responsibilities implied by that relationship. While certainly not the whole story, those schools (usually private) which do have uniform policies, have adopted them as one among a number of tools that help promote the movement toward adulthood. Our public schools, on the other hand, do next to nothing along these lines. Uniforms are a relatively costless way of reversing this trend. Yet I suspect that uniforms have a deeper ideological significance that would stand in the way of their adoption. What is it?

Uniforms point up differences: the outstanding scholar stands out when everyone looks the same

One of the most obvious things about uniforms is that they do something to equalise all who wear them. One would think, therefore, that in this age of egalitarianism an enthusiastic reception for the idea of uniforms might be anticipated. In fact precisely the opposite would occur.

One possible form of objection to uniforms from an egalitarian perspective is the idea that uniforms are *inherently* symbols of upper class status. The extent to which there is any truth in this notion is due to the fact that today one finds uniforms mostly in private schools. Private schools require a payment beyond what one already pays in taxes and thus may generally be the province of the financially better off. But private schools requiring uniforms have certainly existed for the poor in the United States and the bulk of Catholic parochial schools, where uniforms are common, can hardly be said to be schools for the rich.[3]

Uniforms are thus not inherently oriented to any class, however many movies depict upper-crust British or American boarding schools. Yet uniforms are nevertheless not symbols of egalitarianism. Although uniforms do make all children equal with respect to dress, they do nothing to smooth over inequalities in other areas of school and may even serve to highlight them. The scholar or athlete who excels in many ways stands out more in an environment where everyone otherwise looks the same. In contrast, by allowing some to set the pace in fashion, the distinction between what is really meritorious and what is not, is blurred; for we are all aware that the 'cool' dresser is as admired, if not more so, as the superior scholar and perhaps even the superior athlete. Consequently, by failing to remove dress as a source of distinction, the school has effectively sanctioned its equality with other forms of distinction.

The point here extends beyond the school context alone. Uniforms may equalise the rich and the poor children at school. They do not, however, smooth out the inequalities that exist outside of school. How often has it been the case that one student visits the home of a classmate only to be surprised by the social class of the friend's family that remained otherwise hidden from view. Uniforms, then, can *cover up* those inequalities and therein lies the rub.

If obliterating distinctions of class, status, or wealth is the goal of the egalitarian, one must begin by focusing attention upon them. The rich child, for example, could dress in ways others may not be able to afford; but not wanting to stand out, the child will more likely 'dress down' to a common level in order to avoid being perceived as elitist. Either way, the egalitarian cause has been served for the child is forced to be conscious of his social class relative to that of his classmates. There is only a small step from making the child conscious of a disparity to the claim that such disparities are undeserved. And, of course, since the child *is* a child, his social status *is* undeserved, even if that of his parents is not. Consequently, a disposition has begun to be developed within the child to regard all social distinctions as being on a par with distinctions of dress, which is to say, essentially trivial. It is thus *without* uniforms that adult social distinctions and concerns can be brought into the school system and used for political ends. Uniforms, by contrast, simply do not allow any manifestations of adult status or class to be relevant in the relations students have with each other.[4] That, of course, means that status *can* be enjoyed or considered quite relevant in other contexts.

Uniforms offend against multiculturalism's dogma of diversity for its own sake

Egalitarians these days are also likely to oppose uniforms because they are discriminatory and assimilative. The uniformed child is not just integrated into a school—that can just as well be done without uniforms—but is assimilated into it. The uniform is a way of saying to the child that he is now a part of the culture of *that* school and no other. Assimilation stands in contrast to the current call for 'diversity' and 'multiculturalism'. Children left to themselves are not very likely, obviously, to wear the dress of their ancestral cultures, but if they were to do so, it would be necessary to point out that native dress was always a way of *discriminating* one's own culture from another's. Native dress did not celebrate diversity but rather conformity, identity, and exclusion. What is going on in multi-culturalism has little to do with a real celebration of distinctiveness and more to do with an attempt to juxtapose, in a non-judgmental way, diverse 'lifestyles' and thus to effectively level all differences. The trivial and the significant sources of difference become equal under multi-culturalism.

Requiring uniforms would not go so far as native dress with respect to discrimination and assimilation, but they would make the expression of diversity for its own sake impossible. Uniforms would further seem to imply that diversity is simply not appropriate to every context. School is one context where diversity is particularly inappropriate, for the prospects of success in any society at large depend much more on assimilation by means of the acquisition of appropriate educational levels than they do on expressions of diversity.[5]

In sum, although uniforms provide the prospect of equality in many ways, I suspect that the present egalitarian climate would not be favourably disposed to them. The main reason for this is that the egalitarian is committed to an ideology of total equality, and the limited sort provided by uniforms can actually highlight rather than remove certain inequalities.

The moral psychology of uniforms: they teach children the difference between conformity in the trivial and the important

One thing is clear about uniforms, children would prefer not to wear them. What then are the psychological ramifications of forcing them to do so? There shall be no pretence that what follows is a 'scientific' discourse on the psychological effects of wearing uniforms. Rather, I wish to explore the *moral* psychology of the issue. What, in other words, are the psychological components as they might affect moral conduct, or what sorts of moral dispositions are habituated by wearing uniforms? Answers to such questions are quite accessible to the layman, which, however, is not to suggest that further systematic research would not be illuminating.

If children would prefer not to wear uniforms, it follows that wearing them represses certain of their desires. It cannot be the case that repression of a child's desires is bad in itself. Even the most liberal of parents frustrate the desires of their children at times. And although it may not be so evidently practised these days, especially among many well-to-do parents, it is still a sound principle of child-rearing to suggest that children should not be spoiled. It must therefore be the type of desire that is repressed or inhibited that matters, although it must be noted that whatever type it is, uniforms inhibit it on a *systematic* basis.

What is evident upon reflection, is that the type of desires repressed by uniforms tends to conflict directly with those that people today wish to encourage. Complete relativism with respect to dress is encouraged under the rubric of 'self-expression'. Self-expression in this context, however, is clearly not possible with uniforms. Of course, as we have seen, such relativism in no way guarantees an actual diversity of appearance. But outward appearance is not the issue anyway. The issue is whether self-expression in this area is worthy of encouragement.

Children need to be made aware of the difference between the trivial and the substantive. In addition, they must eventually recognise that what is trivial is not necessarily unworthy of concern. Dress is both trivial and worthy of attention, but children cannot distinguish between what is trivially important and what is substantively important. What uniforms do, therefore, is to repress desires for the trivial in favour of desires for the substantive. It is difficult to learn this lesson under circumstances of complete freedom of dress, because the lesson involves first identifying one's desire to dress as one pleases as objectively trivial. However, children, and perhaps even many adults, are likely to determine the trivial on the basis of the *strength* of their desires, not the quality of their objectives. Since they would have a stronger desire for freedom of dress than say mathematics, they would systematically fail to differentiate between the trivial and the substantive. If, by contrast, all works well with the use of uniforms, the child can safely be allowed to indulge his tastes in dress because he has been previously conditioned to understand its relative unimportance.

The attitudinal climate of today, however, fosters exactly the opposite set of priorities among children. Free self-expression is allowed in trivial things, but not substantive ones. One can dress as one likes, but not regard one's accomplishments as the basis for a superior sense of worth. This in turn mirrors the adult world where we have complete freedom in matters of taste, but increasingly less freedom in more significant matters. One has less freedom to determine what to do with one's business or income, for example, than say, one's form of entertainment. Indeed, it is a characteristic part of the welfare state that substantive matters (e.g., one's health care, old age, insurance, education, etc.) are removed from the realm of personal responsibility, leaving to that realm only the trivial. Uniforms suggest a time when people did not mind conformity in trivial matters, because their attention was necessarily directed to the substantive.

Uniforms have the advantage all rules have: they can be relaxed on occasions

The moral psychology of uniforms is also tied to the idea that there can be special events—events which gain significance by at least being out of a routine. Most schools that have uniforms also have special days when they need not be worn. Such days range from 'field days' to simply days off from having to wear them. One school, with which I am familiar, uses non-uniform days to motivate classes in raising money for a school project or other worthy cause. Grades five through eight, for example, might compete with one another in completing some project, with the winning class being allowed to go without their uniform for a day. Not only does this promote a competitive spirit, but it also allows status to be displayed as it should be, on moral grounds—that is, on the basis of some merit. Going without a uniform in this context not only gives the winners a visible sign of success, but it also evokes a certain amount of jealousy and admiration among those who did not win. Although egalitarians may eschew such incentives, their benefits are certainly arguable. In any case, putting something on one's person as a form of differentiation (e.g., a star or arm band) cannot have the same motivating effect as being allowed to take the uniform off. This is because the desire to wear a star can never be as constant and forceful as the desire to be free of one's uniform.

Uniforms teach the acceptance of a degree of tedium

Moreover, even in those cases where the only reason for a special day without a uniform is as relief from the tedium, that point is itself something children need to understand. Life is not constant excitement. Indeed, the real world is full of routines and tediums more demanding than wearing a uniform. Learning to cope with that reality, as well as increasing the appreciation of the true value of those moments when it is relieved, is part of an important lesson too seldom taught these days.

Uniforms humiliate—or rather allow only that self-esteem that is based on achievement

It must also be noted in this context that uniforms are somewhat demeaning. The military has known this aspect of wearing uniforms for a long time. Uniforms were employed as part of a technique to humble new recruits.

With respect to children, nothing could seem more contrary to the current culture of 'self-esteem' than to employ the demeaning technique of having to wear uniforms. Yet self-esteem devoid of accomplishment is no real self-esteem at all. Where uniforms are present, unless one distinguishes oneself by accomplishing something of worth, one is nothing but another student, a nobody, a mere member of the herd. That may be demeaning, but it is also likely to spur on some real accomplishment and self-worth.

A general point can be made by noting that, in so far as uniforms have a role to play in moral training, it is by a method of inhibition. Desires are inhibited in the service of other, more important ends such as the development of character. Habituating oneself by learning to repress or channel one's desires is useful training for children.[6] It is useful training on the supposition that moral action ought to be rooted in personal responsibility and grounded in character. These are the sorts of qualities that depend more on inhibition than exhibition. They suggest that one is responsible and free when one has moulded one's character by channelling and inhibiting one's desires rather than giving vent to them. To link self-expression to outward appearance is to admit that there is no inner self or character to express.

Conclusion

If we lived in a Soviet-style culture, this chapter may have been written in defence of freedom of dress. In that kind of society, what children may need to learn are the benefits of any form of individuality. In our society, however, the problem is now almost equally severe in the other direction. We have not only lost all sense of connection between ethics and character, but are in danger in the United States, as possibly in Britain too, of losing our heritage of individual initiative, individual responsibility, and individual liberty—all of which are rooted the concept of character formation that uniforms played a small role in developing. It is an odd paradox that these sorts of values can be given some support by what appears to be opposed to them. Uniforms may not be the most significant of human concerns, yet in a context where all values are equally relativised, a little thing may go a long way.

CHAPTER 6

The End
of
Authority
and
Formality:

And Their Replacement by Intrusive Regulation

Kenneth Minogue

Authority sick to death

Authority was left for dead in the student revolution of the 1960s and it remains on the sick list. The revolutionaries of that time thought reason could liberate us from the judgement of elders. Like most liberations, this one has had mixed consequences, many of them bitter. Violence at the workplace has, according to a study by Incomes Data Services, risen by 100 per cent in the ten years to 1991. Employers, reported *The Times* in July 1994, blamed 'drug and alcohol abuse, increased defiance of authority, and a climate which suggests that anyone wearing a uniform has become a target'. A uniform is, of course, one visible sign of someone with authority: that is its point. The three reasons given are thus two: drugs, and loss of authority.

Can authority ever recover the important place it once had in our moral life? The answer will be determined by invisible currents of taste and sensibility we cannot guess at, but the one thing we can do is try to understand the place it did once have in our moral universe.

Authority and the principle of hierarchy: offensive to egalitarians

Authority is a hierarchical principle. It accords rule to the higher over the lower, and thus collides with our basic egalitarian sentiments. What people today instinctively ask is: what is someone doing giving orders who is no better than the rest of us—even if he does have a uniform? This attitude clearly affects even the paradigm case of authority: that which descends from the sovereign power of a democratically elected state. A generalised antipathy to policemen as those who frustrate wilfulness carries over, in disorderly parts of the country, into abuse of firemen, soldiers, ambulance drivers, and others associated with civil order. Yet no one in practice doubts the importance of this order, except perhaps for a few anarchists who think the sovereign state itself an evil that must be abolished. Disorderly parts of the country are not residences of choice.

Life once suffused with authority—in families, work, clubs, churches

The range of authority in our lives is, of course, vastly greater than this. It is, indeed, the very texture of the life we live. We grow to adulthood subject to the authority of our parents, of teachers, of the officials of clubs and churches, and in a highly derivative sense, of experts and even journalists. In all of these cases, the holder of authority can implicitly claim greater wisdom or knowledge than those over whom it is exercised. Members of parliament have authority because we have elected them to represent us, but they too share in some degree this derivative cognitive authority arising from knowledge and experience—in their case, knowledge of the intricacies of legislation.

Authority obeyed because it knows best or because obedience is better than the confusion of constant challenge

That we generally obey an authoritative command without cavilling is a convenience in our social life. When a uniformed policeman beckons, one usually obeys without demanding an explanation. We assume that the authority figure knows something we don't; and even if he doesn't, we may well recognise a situation in which it is probably better to have *some* ordering principle rather than confusion. Urgency means that the individual who demands the reason for a direction may well be a pest. It is indeed sometimes the case that the intractable individual holding things up by demanding reasons of authority is not a tedious crank, but 'has a point'. Much more commonly, however, one is wise to give authority the benefit of the doubt in all trivial cases, and the reason is central to the entire logic of the concept of authority.

One can always give reasons for authority in general, but one can seldom give entirely adequate reasons for any particular decision made by an authority. The point is that if one *could* give entirely conclusive reasons, then authority would not be needed. The decision would be rational, and rational decisions (however rare) are beyond argument. Authority is necessary precisely because the something that must be done, or the policy that must be agreed, is unknown, or contested, and it is better to have an authoritative decision than none at all.

Authority of its nature vulnerable to those who demand reasons: it rests on practice and convenience

This makes authority peculiarly vulnerable to those who demand reasons. University vice-chancellors in the 1960s opened and shut their mouths like distressed fish when students 'questioned' the reasons for the most basic features of academic institutions. No one for centuries had given much thought to committee structures or disciplinary procedures, nor to whether or not universities should have any particular set of facilities.

The reasons for what was inherited from the past lay deeply embedded in the practices themselves. Universities are no doubt places where everything ought to be open to inquiry, but (like everything human) they ultimately rest merely upon what generations of members have found it convenient to do. Academics in the 1960s, however, found themselves like parents victimised by aggressive tots forever repeating the question 'why?' as a response to the last explanation. Most parents end by using 'shut up' as the best explanation; the kindlier ones say: 'because I say so'. Aggressive ideologists in their twenties were harder to fob off with such replies. Anything less than a capitulation to their demands was stigmatised as being 'authoritarian' and that term reveals much about the decline of the idea of authority. All it can legitimately mean is the use of authority as a pseudo-reason in circumstances in which it is appropriate to give a real reason. Most commonly it refers to what these days is called a 'confrontational' manner used by an officeholder in dealing with those over whom he has authority.

Authority currently seen as the opposite of freedom yet it only stops us doing what we should not

It is revealing that in time, 'authoritarian' grew out of this merely adverbial role and became an adjective designating a special kind of 'personality' which explained the success of totalitarian regimes. In the famous Milgram experiments, many subjects seemed to prefer obeying an authority figure in a white coat to ceasing to press buttons which (they had been told) were causing agony to unseen subjects in the next room. Authority in a repressive society, it seemed, deformed decency.

This line of argument suggests that authority and freedom are opposites. Authority on some occasions impedes us from doing what we might be inclined to do. On the other hand, authority legitimately exercised would only frustrate what we ought *not* to do. The deep issue here is how we conceive of ourselves as human beings. If we are simply bundles of inclinations, and frustration is the worst thing that can happen, then authority does indeed frustrate. But if we recognise moral channels of conduct along which we must pursue whatever it is we desire, then authority merely keeps us doing the right thing.

As authority declines, regulations increase

It does so with a relatively light touch. The proof of this lies in the paradox that the more authority declines in our society as a ubiquitous part of the texture within which we live, legislation and regulation expand, along with an exploding apparatus of inspectors, arbitrators, regulators, licensors, social workers, customs officials, taxation clerks, and many others who acquire the power to impose regulations upon us. Whether they are preferable to the authority of teachers, fathers, clergymen, etc., is a matter of judgement.

Hamlet was well aware of the insolence of office, and few have not experienced it. Insolence results from the fact that authority rests upon power. Police and armies sustain the authority of states, while parents are stronger than their children. Their authority, indeed, may not outlast the erosion of this condition. Even the irritating clerk who makes difficult some transaction may have the discretion to withhold something we want. These facts keep alive our awareness that civil and social authority historically derives from conquest, and that the authoritativeness of the holders of authority is now the sediment of custom left behind by the violence of yesteryear. In the days when authority was raw power, only the courageous dared to challenge it, and some who did paid for their temerity with their lives. Today, authority is muffled in procedure, and challenging it is like twisting the tail of a toothless and feeble old lion. Children do it to boast a fantasy courage.

Authority thought unnecessary except in unusual circumstances

But real power, even that of conquerors, is subject in the long run to the erosion of ideas. Authority as a principle has succumbed to a false idea, namely that social order is basically spontaneous. This false idea generalises the common experience that we only need a policeman on exceptional occasions. People work or play together for the most part without having to think of the conditions which make it possible. It is only when they become violent that we hear the wail of sirens. These facts have often led simple empiricists to believe that human beings are naturally peaceful and orderly, and that the force of the state, far from being a remedy for disorder, as widely touted, is, rather, the actual cause of individuals themselves resorting to force and violence in their dealings with others.

Alternatively, it is argued by socialists that violence results from an unjust society in which some are rich and some are poor. In all such theories, any distinction between rulers and ruled, indeed even any *need* for the distinction, is thought to reveal a defect in the way society has been constructed. Hierarchy thus violates the principle that all men are equal, and that my desires and my judgements are, in principle, no less worth attending to than those of others.

Opponents of authority would replace it with negotiation: that might mean chaos and crime

Authority in these terms is a relic of a bad past. It ought to be replaced by discussion between rational individuals. It ought to be replaced, in fact, by negotiation. As models of social harmony, the army gives way to the Quaker prayer meeting. Social harmony is possible without authority. The question then becomes: is this realistic?

The most powerful denial of this view is to be found in the *Leviathan* of Thomas Hobbes, published in 1651 after Britain had been ravaged by a civil war costing about 100,000 lives. Hobbes argued that a sovereign power was necessary because human beings were in competition for scarce things in the world, were quarrelsome because others did not take them at their own valuation, and were aggressive because they feared the aggression of others. All the achievements of civilization ultimately resulted from reliance on sovereign authority. The novelist William Golding presented a brilliant image of this view of the human condition in his novel *Lord of the Flies*. It is true, of course, that those entrusted with supreme authority may indeed misuse it, and that power corrupts. But it is also true that terrible things happen without authority, from the scale of disasters in Africa and Asia as authority breaks down to street corner crime.

Authority contrasted with the power to command

Certainly the Roman originators of the idea of authority would not have found it difficult to recognise Hobbes' account of the human condition. *Auctoritas* was the quality attaching to an author or *auctor*, and was supremely illustrated by the veneration accorded Romulus, the notional founder of the city. Romulus was reputed to have appointed a number of distinguished families to sustain his design for Rome, and authority incarnated in the

Senate flowed down from one generation to the next. It was not a difficult idea for the Romans because each Senator was himself an *auctor* within his own family, either founding or continuing his own family. Even the writers of books, as *auctors*, had a certain authority in their interpretation. Christianity adopted this idea of the authority of a founder in the position accorded to Jesus in the Christian religion. *Auctoritas* for the Romans was a quality making them take pronouncements seriously; it was not the same thing as the command of an official, who possessed the different quality of *potestas*. This distinction was passed on to European politics by the usages of the Catholic Church. The British, who might claim to be a little more like the Romans than some other European peoples, followed Rome in creating a society thickly textured with authority. England was full of 'gouvenors'— nobles, teachers, clergymen, employers, heads of families, and so on. Sir Thomas Elyot's book of advice to them, published in 1531, was a notable best seller.

The loss of a widely diffused, practically based authority

Authority in England went with a talent for spontaneous order which foreigners admired from at least the 18th century onwards. The English were deferential to authority, and knew their place. Children attending public schools were trained for 'leadership', which meant the skill of recreating order after a breakdown. This is easier if there are people recognisable by social signs who bear the responsibility for it. All of these expressions today provoke derision, and together they suggest that England was a caste society. Nothing could be further from the truth. Competence remained in all cases the basic test of the exercise of authority, as in the kind of situation turned into romance by J. M. Barrie in *The Admirable Crichton*, in which one of those masterful butlers common in English fiction becomes the boss when the family is shipwrecked on a desert island. The reason is he knows better how to handle the situation. Social mobility in Britain in recent times is about the same as in other countries. Nor has the rate of mobility much changed since the moral revolution of the 1960s, when authority was defenestrated. All that has happened is the growth of a certain breezy self-confidence, call it 'swagger', by which people take the limits of their own understanding for the values of the world. Civility began to decline because sloppy pronunciation made it sound like 'servility'.

Authority and the First World War

The decline of authority is the most portentous thing that has happened to Britain, and perhaps to Western civilization, in this century. In the British case particularly, the First World War is the crucial event. It has entered legend as being not only savagely costly in lives, but as being unnecessarily so. The idea that the 'donkeys' who led the 'lions' in those doomed advances on the Western Front were simply 'upper class twits' transformed the moral attitudes of many. That the supposed donkeys actually won suggests that we ought to reserve a certain scepticism for this view of the past, but there is little doubt about its consequences.

Indeed, the legend of the First World War may well be the consequence no less than the cause of the deeper changes which were transforming the Western view of society. The idea of democracy, burrowing down from politics into social attitudes, was hostile to the notion that the right to command should be based on anything else but ability, if that. But that very proposition gets the whole question on to the wrong footing. For if there actually is a technical question which can be answered by an expert, then authority is either irrelevant, or else is authoritative merely in a derived sense. To understand this point requires that we should disentangle the basic idea of authority from some of its semantic derivatives.

Two different authorities: that of the expert and that of those authorised to act for us

The historiography of the middle ages written by liberals made much of the uncritical habit of resting belief on authority. Only intellectual donkeys (or possibly Buridan's ass) believed things merely because they had been reported in earlier books. The thing was to think for oneself. But as the philosopher Karl Popper most recently pointed out, nearly everything that we believe has been acquired by this process. We test very little by our own experience. Academic authorities, then, are quite rightly entitled to our deference, even though we obviously have the right to inquire and challenge anything we think worth querying. In academic argument, authority is a useful guide but never decisive.

These various considerations reveal that there are two quite distinct kinds of authority: the authority of those believed to be expert or knowledgeable, and the authority of those (such as the sovereign rulers of a country) who have this character basically because *we* have authorised them to act for us. And we must recognise that this second kind of authority cannot at all be replaced by experts, and that anyone purporting to be an expert in this area must be a mountebank. We may call the first *expert* authority (which includes academic experts) and the second *practical* authority. And in setting up this

71

dichotomy, I have used 'practical' in preference to 'political' because practical authority is to be found both formally in the institutions of the state, and *informally* in any situation where people may be confused or in doubt, and look to others for guidance about how to proceed.

Practical authority and the avoidance of pointless disputes—family life without parental authority

Informal practical authority is the texture of authority within which we all live and the propensity to recognise it is the mark of a civilized person. I am told that the rather sexist Chinese symbol of 'conflict' pictures two women under the same roof, and the plausibility of this image lies in the fact that in any practical activity, such as cooking, there must be one guiding intelligence, one, that is, who has authority. Without such a convention, there will be endless pointless disputes. Our inherited family structure had fathers as the notional heads of families, a situation which allowed in practice a good deal of delegated authority to wives and elder children. No doubt this convention of authority subjected many families to the petty tyranny of tiresome fathers, but its overthrow in our generation, while no doubt liberating some families from tyranny, has liberated others from family life altogether. In this, as in every social arrangement, there are advantages and disadvantages to every option we try. The decline of family solidarity thus brings us back to the pregnant theme of why the whole sense of authority has declined.

The waning of authority: the challenge to distance and formality

We have seen that events, such as the First World War, interpreted as failures of strategy, and principles, such as equality and democracy, have eroded authority. There are also deeper currents of moral experience to be recognised, most notably the decline of the practice of *distance* between individuals. The sign of distance was formality. Titles (such as Mr. and Mrs.) and manners allowed individuals to associate together without too closely becoming intimate. It may seem, in these times when 'community' is the watchword of a satisfactory life, and 'alienation' the common description of our miseries, that a practice of distance could only be perverse. What makes it sensible is that human consciousness is confused and chaotic, and that the posture of rationality we present to the world is an achievement. Hobbes believed that:

The most sober men, when they walk alone without care and employment of the

72

mind, would be unwilling the vanity and extravagance of their thoughts at that time should be publicly seen; which is a confession, that passions unguided, are for the most part mere madness.

(Leviathan, Ch. 8)

Formal dress, formal speech, formal topics of social exchange (such as the weather) have in the past allowed Europeans (and especially the English) to create a society in which both freedom and individuality could flourish because each person had the privacy within which to develop his or her own thoughts, and to cultivate inclinations and passions. Individualities of this kind had no difficulty with informal authority because it did not press upon their inner lives. All that authority requires is that one should fit into some scheme for the time being; it does not require belief or enthusiasm.

A case study in the decline of authority: child-centred education

The rise of child-centred education illustrates the way in which individuality and authority are linked together. Traditional education required the pupil to obey the teacher, and his understanding was authoritatively guided by the teacher so as to respond to a recognised literature—the classical writers, the skills of mathematics, historical narratives, geographical structures, and so on. Child-centred education took its bearings from the supposed inclinations of the child himself. The repressive hand of authority, as it seemed, was to be replaced by the spontaneous curiosity of the child. What happened in practice, however, was a much more intimate involvement of the teacher in the inner life of the child, diminishing the space within which the child might think his own thoughts unguided. Even more significantly, it involved the teacher *manipulating* the child's inclinations, because it was, after all, necessary that by the end of the process of education, the child should have acquired most of the skills traditionally required.

Authority required formal compliance: what has replaced it is much more intrusive

It was Plato's belief that social change basically begins in the dark recesses of family life, and we may follow this clue in accounting for the decline in the idea of authority. For the child first meets this idea in responding to the commands of parents in the little despotism of family life. But authority depends on distance. Further, with the rise of the welfare state, children become less the necessary props of old age and symbol of social continuity than consumer objects that we like to enjoy. But in egalitarian times, exercising authority is a requirement that collides with our desire for intimacy and friendship with our children. The parent seeking to be the friend of the child necessarily forfeits authority. As this egalitarian drive works itself out, indeed, children of quite a young age come increasingly under the jurisdiction of the state, exercising its suasion through social workers, and they acquire rights which make it increasingly difficult for either teachers or parents to exercise authority. Social workers gain power at the expense of both parents and policemen. But just as there are ineluctable necessities about what the child must end up by knowing, so in the family there are ineluctable necessities for familial peace and harmony. If authority can no longer be exercised, how are these necessities to be achieved? The straightforward answer is: by negotiation. Benefits must be exchanged—in terms of pocket money, night time curfews, television rights, the giving and receiving of love, etc. Children and parents thus become power players negotiating with each other on more or less equal terms about what shall be given and received.

Authority replaced by negotiation which depends on manipulation

This example brings out the basic fact about the decline of authority: that it involves the rise of manipulation. If you cannot rule children, you must fool them, taking the risk, of course, that they will fool you. On the grander political stage the decline of authority as a limited principle of social and political life is paralleled by the rise of manipulative and regulatory politics, in which more and more areas of life must be subject to rules and, when contested, brought before courts and tribunals whose decisions, in spite of the elaborate codes by which they are governed, are increasingly arbitrary. What is most remarkable is how little we have learned from an experience which exhibited not only the decline but the actual abolition of authority. This was the experience of Communist totalitarianism. Communists ruled the Soviet Union not because they had been delegated authority by the people, but because they possessed the true doctrine of how a society must be organised. They possessed reason, not mere authority, and reason turned out to be not just oppressive but false and homicidal. In three generations, little trace remained of individuality and nothing was left of communal solidarity.

European society: the combination of individuality, authority, formality, and intimacy

Human beings are flexible creatures, but without manners and morals they become brittle. The great strength of European societies has been their individuality which depended, as I have argued, upon a sense of distance from each other. It is precisely this sense of distance which accounts for romance and chivalry in the West, for those whom manners keep apart retain a capacity for intimacy unknown to those whose sense of formality has been destroyed. As St. Augustine observed of poetry, it is the discipline of formality which intensifies passion. One can only love as an individual, but with the decline of authority, few now understand individuality. It is foolishly thought to be merely will, the set of demands made by an individual on the circle of those about him. In 1994, the Archbishop of Canterbury was reported to be discussing with bishops something called 'excessive individuality', which can only mean that individuality is merely demandingness and must adjust to the thing called 'society'. Self-interest, which is a moral duty in a modern society, comes to be identified with the vice of selfishness.

The law of modern life is that moral decline, amplified by journalistic indignation, generates regulation, which in turn accentuates the moral decline, which in turn produces demands for more regulation, and so on. In the middle of the 20th century, we still enjoyed a conception of civil authority in which Dixon of Dock Green or Officer Krupke could keep order on their beat by a raised finger and, no doubt on occasion, by a clip across the ear. These men could exercise authority because they knew that authority has its limits. But the decline of authority may not only be a collapse of respect for officers, but also a decline of people who can be trusted to exercise it. The police are now closely regulated because many of them are individualities in the debased modern sense, that is to say, people conscious of little else but their own inclinations. They cannot always be trusted to exercise the self-discipline which moderates the passions.

Violence and power may be necessary to restore authority

The decline of authority is a theme so large that it would be absurd to suggest policies to reverse the trend. The only thing one can say with confidence is that nearly every regulation or codification designed to correct it will destroy the spontaneous moral responses that may begin to improve our situation. The really alarming truth is that authoritative order had first to be established by power and violence before it could solidify into the custom of authority, and that in the end its decline may only be halted by the recurrence of those conditions.

CHAPTER 7

Ostracism and Disgrace in the Maintenance of a Precarious Social Order

Daniel Lapin

The natural state of human society—like the universe—is chaos

The laws of physics contain many elegant analogies to principles of human behaviour. This comes as no surprise to an Orthodox rabbi, who believes that one God created both the physical and human worlds, and the laws that apply to each. The monotheistic traditions, beginning with Judaism, teach that God's act of creation preceded, and transcended, the physical laws that we know today. Without His intervention, the universe remains captive to the first law of thermodynamics: entropy is always increasing. In other words, defeating entropy is a God-like act. While only He can reverse entropy at the universal level, we humans can at least create small oases of physical and spiritual light. These oases, our neighbourhoods, communities, and other associations, provide a valuable framework for our lives. Building them fights entropy, and is a worthy pursuit for beings made in God's image. All humans who strive to act in imitation of God, then, will consider maintaining such oases their principal vocation. In this chapter I will first explore the magnitude of the difficulty humans encounter in fighting entropy. I will then discuss some weapons the English-speaking world once used successfully in this battle, and explain why those weapons have been left to rust in padlocked armouries.

Contemplate first the depressing finality of entropy. I take a large glass jar, and fill it with neatly arranged rows of red and green marbles. I cover the jar and shake it. We observe the marbles vibrating and migrating round the jar until, pretty soon, all signs of the original layered pattern have vanished. How long must I shake the jar so as to have the marbles return to their original layers? Consider: each marble can occupy only a finite number of positions in the jar, and all the marbles of the same colour are interchangeable. I do not require any marble to return to its original place. In fact, I can drastically reduce my expectations, and remove the requirement that the original pattern be replicated. I will accept columns, diagonals—any arrangement of marbles that looks ordered rather than random. How long could it take to shake these miserable marbles into some conformance with my requirements? And yet, order simply refuses to emerge out of chaos. This is a real mystery.

Consider another example of the same law. Suppose we leave an automobile in a field for a few centuries, then return to inspect the result. What do we find? A heap of iron oxide, some powdered glass, bits of rubber, and so forth. If we attempt to reverse the experiment, leaving the decomposed materials and checking every hundred years or so to see if nature has reconstructed a car, we will remain disappointed for ever. We are so accustomed to these processes that we ignore the staggering mystery: why on earth should a car spontaneously break down into its component parts, but those same parts never recombine into a car? The entropy principle explains that a kind of natural gravity is at work. It tends to pull things down into their lowest state of order. The marbles will never return to an ordered arrangement, no matter how long or vigorously I shake them. Entropy keeps them in random and chaotic arrangements. An automobile is a most carefully contrived arrangement of glass, iron, plastic, and rubber. Like the marbles, once disarranged, those component parts will never come back together by chance.

Creating and maintaining order requires energy and intellect

The finality of entropy leads us to a consideration of the 'natural'. We see that creating order out of chaos always requires energy and intellect. Maintaining that order requires energy as well. Nature, in this sense, represents the universe without the application of energy or intellect. We all know that the Bible, the founding document of Western civilization, opens with God's conversion of primeval natural chaos into an ordered universe. Because the creation occurs at the very beginning, we understand why the Hebrew word for nature, *teva*, does not appear in the Bible: nature is essentially driven out in the first sentence.

At the pedestrian level of our two entropy examples, we can see that the more natural state is the one with the most chaos and the least amount of intelligent energy. Our unsymmetrical scattering of coloured marbles is natural, layered patterns of marbles are not. Heaps of iron oxide and broken glass are far more natural than a working automobile. Similarly, a stagnant swamp is more natural than a harbour.

A random collection of self-serving brutes is more natural than an advanced society of courteous and compassionate individuals

Now let us consider applying these principles to the human world. We shall investigate whether a random aggregation of self-serving brutes is more natural than an ordered society of courteous and compassionate citizens. For this thought experiment we use the following protocol: we deposit a young boy and a young girl on an otherwise deserted tropical island. Taking care that they have enough to eat, we set up concealed surveillance equipment and observe their development. As time passes, their numbers will increase, until a full-fledged society grows up on the island. Eventually, we may assume that they will notice periodicity in the heavens, discovering a 365¼-day solar year, and a lunar month of roughly 30 days. However, it is highly unlikely that they will develop a seven-day week. Astronomy reveals no seven-day cycle, and seven does not divide evenly into either 30 or 365. This makes the seven-day week a very illogical choice; five days would make more sense—and think of all the paper they could save on calendars, since every year would be an exact replica of the preceding one.

Why, then, does our society have something as confusing and artificial as a seven-day week, when switching to five would be so logical? Only because we retain a primeval, collective memory: that God ordained a seven-day cycle as a kind of divine Circadian rhythm. In other words, if human society on Earth had evolved without divine guidance, as in our tropical island thought experiment, it would be hard to account for the wide acceptance of the seven-day week.

Many of our traditions, our family structures, and manners not linked to human inventiveness

Similarly, our experimental society might eventually discover steam power, electricity, and even nuclear energy. (I subscribe to the belief that major intellectual advances are driven by a religious impulse, but, for the purposes of the thought experiment, we will assume the advances will occur.) But how would they discover and establish manners? There is nothing to suggest that scratching oneself in public, or allowing one's body to emit loud noises, is intrinsically wrong. Far more likely, people would simply become accustomed to, and ignore, such behaviour. Would monoga-

81

mous marriage and the nuclear family emerge as the normative social arrangement? No—why should it? It is not readily apparent that men can best satisfy their own interests by submitting to the restrictions of monogamy. And so on, down the list of humanity's moral and social conventions. While intellectual capacity is clearly built into the brain, certain fundamental patterns of civilization are much less obviously linked to human inventiveness. Attributing the origin of these patterns to divine guidance seems very reasonable indeed.

Since, by hypothesis, our island community has developed without such guidance, we should not expect its scientific development to have produced a corresponding level of social refinement. I maintain that the island, in its post-industrial phase, would more closely resemble the Rwandan civil war than it would small-town America in 1955. Indeed, the etiology of decadence, from the Bible to Gibbon, to Spengler, has remained remarkably predictable. This is the best explanation of why the nation that produced Goethe, Beethoven, and the prince of physics, Max Planck, could also be the people that gave us Auschwitz. There is no inherent contradiction, and it could have happened almost anywhere. It took some very special moral energy to produce the social order of the British Empire or of American civilization. Germany lost that energy, and our island experiment never had it.

The question is not what has caused our lives to become so squalid, costly, and dangerous, but what did we used to do that kept society so safe, prosperous, and stable?

Our thought experiment reveals that our normal question about the decline of civilization has the order of things backward. We usually ask, 'What has caused our lives to become so much more squalid, expensive and dangerous?' Instead, we should be asking, 'What did we used to do that kept society so stable, safe, and prosperous?' To use another analogy, don't ask what made the aeroplane tumble out of the sky. The answer is simple—it ran out of fuel. Ask rather where the fuel came from and how it was converted into the thrust that kept the craft in the air.

Similarly, when studying social decay, the question is not what brought foul-mouthed louts to menace shoppers in our malls. Instead, the critical questions are these: why was a visitor to a theatre or department store in the 1950s surrounded by neatly dressed people who exuded politeness and consideration? Why, back then, were our buses, parks, and other public places safe at all hours of the night? What made most young people marry and raise children responsibly? That was the miracle; what we see now is nature.

The fuel that used to keep the aeroplane of society airborne has run out. We are plummeting earthwards. Instead of an altimeter in the cockpit, we have statistics on growing rates of illegitimacy. Instead of the queasy feeling in the stomach that comes from dropping too rapidly, we have the discomfort of sharing our streets, stores, and parks with unmannered, angry, inconsiderate, obscene, sinister thugs. Like the whirling dial of the altimeter, illegitimacy should more urgently claim our attention; we should realise how close we have come to hitting the ground. However, back in the passenger cabin, we are more aware of our churning insides. In our daily lives, it is the many small shocks to the system that we endure, that convince us we are in trouble. Sometimes it is the screamed insult and raised finger from another car at a real or imagined driving error. It can be riding on the subway and being subjected to overwhelmingly loud speech peppered with obscenities that would have made a hardened convict blush only a generation ago. Nearly always, it is fear.

The armoury by which civil society used to be maintained—disgrace and ostracism

So how did we once maintain a society that was a model of prosperity, tranquillity, and politeness? The answer is that we employed several fundamental moral weapons which we have now become too timid to use (at least in this context). These weapons include disapproval, ostracism, and other sanctions. The teenage girl who became pregnant was sent away to have the baby. The shame she brought on herself and her family was deep and lasting. In addition, the bastard child carried the disgrace throughout his life, with diminished career and marriage prospects.

As we approach the end of the millennium, enlightened liberals tend to throw up their hands in horror at the thought that ostracism and moral censure should be put to such barbaric uses. To them, I appear to be advocating the wholesale slaughter of civil rights. I would argue to the contrary, on three grounds. First, I suggest that the traditional use of ostracism and censure educated society on the proper ties between people, God, and community, while the abandonment of these tools has led to a rampant and dangerous individualism. Secondly, I maintain that proper and judicious use of social sanctions prevents far more problems than it creates—as do many other forms of punishment. Thirdly, I show that no community can succeed without ostracism and censure, and that the liberals' own use of these tools (when it suits them) amply proves the point.

It may be justified to stigmatise children

In the 'resolution of censure' which society once passed on the unwed mother, the modern liberal objects most vociferously to the clause which ostracizes the bastard. Even if the mother deserves her punishment, goes the liberal line, what possible justification can society have for attainting an innocent child, who certainly did nothing to deserve the stigma? A traditional answer to this takes us back to the story of Noah. *Genesis* 9:20-27 relates how Noah's son Ham sinned by viewing his father's nakedness, then bragging of it to his brothers. Interestingly, when Noah wakens, and determines to mete out punishment, he curses not Ham, the miscreant, but Ham's son Canaan.

Noah realised two critical facts about the human condition which escape the notice of modern liberals. First, he saw that civilization depends upon maintaining a 'community of the generations'. Everything we do affects the generations to come, and either honours or dishonours our ancestors. Even in our egalitarian society, we know that our positive achievements and our monetary success benefit our children. Why should we expect that our sins will not harm them? Indeed, Noah's second, and related insight, was that people care more about their loved ones than about themselves. Men will always sacrifice themselves for their wives, and brothers for their sisters. But even stronger is the mother's instinct to protect her children. Far from an act of injustice, the ostracism of a bastard is a gesture of profound respect for the mother-child tie, the most critical building-block of civilization.

When sanctions are tough, they are rare

The point of social sanctions, like the point of any other deterrence mechanism, is not to ruin lives, but to preserve the common welfare. Anyone urging the return of such sanctions hopes that their very presence will make the occasions for their use quite rare. Back in the 1950s, the number of pregnant schoolgirls who were stigmatized was tiny, and so was the rate of illegitimacy. The number of vagrants who were harassed out of respectable neighbourhoods was minute, and the streets were safe and clean. More recently, the citizens of Kennesaw, Georgia (who passed an ordnance requiring all households to be armed), only had to shoot their first robber. This was obviously unfortunate for that robber; it may even have been unfair, since nothing in his hitherto prosperous career had prepared him for the warm Georgia reception he was given. But he could hardly be described as an innocent bystander.

Ostracism and moral censure can be mild: the case of the business community

It would, however, be a mistake to conceive of social sanctions as merely the spiritual equivalent of a shotgun. One reason ostracism and moral censure are so powerful is that they may be employed in widely varying degrees of intensity. The patterns of the business world reveal how subtle, carefully nuanced, social devices can be just as effective as a scarlet letter. For example, very few companies find the need for written codes of dress, relying on non-verbal communication, and even the occasional use of ostracism (e.g., conspicuously excluding a sloppy dresser from a prestigious luncheon), in achieving a high level of conformity to an established norm. Similarly, business can signal full-fledged acceptance, extreme disapproval, or anything in between, through the judicious application of promotions, pay rises, perquisites, and the like. Even such simple indicators as who is and is not consulted about a decision (another minor form of ostracism) can have a powerful impact on a person's status and respect within a company.

Charitable organisations too, manipulate social status rewards to encourage (and sometimes even intimidate) prospective contributors. Very few non-profit groups can survive without special 'inner circles' of major donors, effectively ostracizing those of insufficient means or inadequate generosity.

Sanctions cannot work in a moral or religious vacuum

A final and most critical point about sanctions: society requires a religious sense of moral conviction in order to authorise their use. 'Noah walked with God', and thus had no qualms about cursing his grandson. Similarly, ostracizing an unwed pregnant teenager and shunning her child requires a Bible-believing, prayerful community. The only way sanctions tough enough to deal with current disorder are going to be effective is if they have supernatural endorsement. Even the radical secularists I discuss below have made a religion out of their secularism. This explains why they often appear unreasonable, even to many who agree with them in principle on particular issues.

The use of ostracism, shame, and other sanctions by liberals: anti-smoking, Political Correctness, and AIDS

Let us now consider whether liberals can legitimately complain about the 'injustice' of ostracism and censure. Any English-speaking person who has read the newspapers or watched television in the past 20 years will quickly see that this question requires virtually no argument. I will offer just three

85

examples of modern liberals' use of social sanctions. We will see that liberals eagerly employ what they profess to eschew, and with the same spiteful relish of a 17th century Puritan stoning an accused witch.

Observe the strangely religious fervour with which liberals attack, for instance, smokers. Anyone who has observed the progress of the anti-smoking movement can see several clear parallels to the most fervent crusades of the Right. First, what began as an effort to curb smoking voluntarily has spilled over into a massively coercive juggernaut that will cost employers billions for pure air in the workplace. Secondly, the Left has blatantly contradicted its own hedonistic individualism, campaigning against smoking by pregnant women and against parents who inflict second-hand smoke on their children. (Can it be that Noah was right: that the welfare of children is the straightest road to the hearts of their parents?) Thirdly, the crusade has extended to attacking the innocent. Gigantic liability judgments against tobacco companies really hurt countless innocent workers whose pension funds depend on the confiscated corporate dividends. The liberals respond to this by repeating platitudes about 'the importance of sending a message', a process they once bitterly denounced—when the message being sent wasn't to their liking.

'Sending a message' is also the justification often used by the campus crusaders for Political Correctness, who have created an entire industry of vilification, using precisely the kinds of social sanctions liberals once claimed to repudiate.

Anyone who requires a third example of this phenomenon should turn on the television during an American awards show (there seems to be one every week). The presenters and recipients, male and female, are beautiful, exquisitely dressed, and meticulously coifed. With equal care (and self-consciousness), they wear red 'AIDS Awareness' ribbons. It takes very little effort to imagine the social pressure these egalitarian aristocrats must feel to wear those ribbons—how else to account for such conformity in an otherwise radically individualistic (not to mention badly behaved) crowd?

Liberals' hypocritical dependence on ostracism and moral censure to uphold their own norms shows that no community can survive without such sanctions. The universality of these social enforcement mechanisms invites the question of how the values to be enforced differ between the modern liberal and the Judeo-Christian traditions.

When stigmatism is acceptable, indeed necessary: the control of appetites

In stark contrast to liberalism, the Judeo-Christian tradition teaches that humans and animals are radically different. Traditionalists believe that manners were ordained by God, and that they serve primarily to enforce the distinction between human and animal. Anyone born in the English-speaking world before 1980 probably had a mother or a grandmother who asked, 'Were you raised on a farm?' following an egregious breach of manners. This concern for the human/animal distinction in turn depends on the religious belief that the unseen, or spiritual world, is more important than the visible, or material world. The Talmud addresses both of these principles by laying down the rule that we must feed our hungry animals before we feed ourselves. This rule directs our attention to the fact that animals necessarily suffer from their relative inability to control their appetites and to anticipate the future. We humans, in contrast, can master the rumblings of our bodies (also called, revealingly, 'animal instincts'), because we are spiritual creatures. A critical technique in the success of liberals, therefore, has been to redirect people's attention from the spiritual to the material, and from the invisible future (or past) to the visible present.

Henry Hazlitt gave us a brilliant example of this technique in his classic tract, *Economics in One Lesson*. In the book's first chapter, a broken pane of glass in a shop window is mis-interpreted by the witnesses as an economic boon. They calculate the stimulative effect on the glass repair man, the increased purchasing power of his wife, etc. Their fallacy, of course, lies in forgetting the correspondingly diminished economic circumstances of the shop owner. The visible and present payment to the glass repair man obscures the invisible and future uses to which the shopkeeper might have put the money. (In only one respect is Hazlitt's book dated: the pane of glass is broken by accident, not maliciously, the event does not touch off a riot or a looting spree, and the bystanders are conspicuously thoughtful and polite.)

Sentimentality and the increase in crime

Similarly, liberals have turned the case of the wrongfully punished individual into a cliché in cinema, theatre, and television. Directing our attention to a present and visible example of injustice, the story line of many a play or film thus conditions us into a dangerous sentimentalism, and away from a broader, more mature concern for society as a whole. As with any breakdown of traditional disciplines, however, the resultant disorder often turns against the tradition-destroyers themselves. The U.S. in the 1990s has seen crime gain and hold first place among the issues of public concern. How did this happen? By removing traditional moral principles from the criminal justice system, the liberals spawned a crime wave that has affected at least one relative or friend of the vast majority of American voters. By also inculcating a sentimentalist spirit in those voters, liberals gave every friend or relative of a crime victim not merely a sense that the system had ill served him, but genuine moral outrage that society had failed in the most important respect. This indignation is now turning against the liberals responsible for creating it—much to their surprise.

It remains to be seen whether the righteous indignation of the traditionalist majority will prevail over the powerful choke-hold which anti-religious liberals continue to maintain on Western culture. As I have endeavoured to show, the various elements in the traditional paradigm of social continuity are critically interdependent. And liberals have assaulted every one of those elements. Radical environmentalists teach our children that man is just another animal, that human uniqueness is a naive prejudice. Behaviourists assault the idea of moral choice, convincing legislators and judges that individuals cannot be held responsible for their actions. The entertainment industry uses rare cases of injustice to condemn the very notion of punishment. All of these attacks are intended to supplant a God-fearing spiritual vision with a God-denying materialist creed. Perhaps the continued vitality of the religious majority, in defiance of such overwhelming odds, is the clearest sign that the secularists are wrong.

CHAPTER 8

Respectability and Approbation:

Ways to Attach Ordinary People to Virtuous Behaviour

Christie Davies

Respectability derided by progressive opinion

Respectability as a means of attaching people to virtue has not had a good press in the last half of the 20th century. Those who continue to use it as a moral compass in their lives are regularly accused of hypocrisy, snobbery, harshness, inflexibility, uncharitableness, smugness, pride, self-righteousness, and mindless conformity. They are subjected to ridicule by progressive writers in literature and the mass media and are rejected and denigrated by hand-wringing social workers anxious not to appear judgmental and punitive, except, of course, when unleashed by their sinister bureaucratic mentors. Raffish aristocrats and hedonistic yuppies, rude proles and sneering intellectuals alike now attack with impunity those who were once seen as the pillars of society: the respectable 'tidy people'. At the very point where the middle classes and the skilled and reliable workers have become a numerical majority in the advanced Western industrial societies, the values and patterns of behaviour known as respectability which were historically associated with these classes have crumbled.

The shame when respectability is lost

About 30 years ago in a medium-sized provincial town in Wales, I remember there being acted out one of the last full-scale dramas of respectability. The son of a widow living in a nearby street was convicted and fined in another town for committing a minor but bizarre sexual offence. His activities as revealed in court were extensively reported in the local newspaper; it had presumably been tipped off by a shrewd, greedy, and callous journalist who knew where the story would sell. Since the deviant one no longer lived in the town, he was not himself exposed to the horrified disapproval of his elders. The people who suffered were his family, namely his widowed mother and the younger children living at home, all of whom were conventionally pious Roman Catholics. For weeks after the press report they would only leave and enter their house by the back door, the informal, unobserved, private exit that emerged into a bumpy ill-kept lane. The official formal door at the front that led into their 'hall' and 'parlour' remained permanently locked. Likewise they ceased visiting the local shops where they were known and travelled into the distant and anonymous town centre. When getting near to home after such a shopping expedition, the mother would huddle deeper into her coat and walk faster with her eyes looking straight ahead yet also resolutely downwards, lest she be accosted by a neighbour aware of her family's recent shameful history. Because of the actions of one absent member of the family, the entire family's reputation had been destroyed and they had no choice but to become socially invisible until such a time as the stigma faded. They had lost their respectability.

It is this kind of true and unfair experience that people have in mind when they condemn respectability as an oppressive means of compelling virtuous conduct. Was it right that this particular family had to suffer so much shame in order that other families and neighbourhoods could be relied on to police the behaviour of their potentially deviant members? Also, in the case that I have described, there is an obsession with sexual misdemeanour unpleasantly like that of the politically correct witch-finders who probe into private lives and private conversations in order to find evidence for mendacious and hysterical accusations of sexual harassment. They too are often in league with a prurient and greedy press that thrives on scandal. Yet in point of fact the forces of respectability of the past often sought to avoid open scandal, respected privacy, and even hushed matters up, which is why a concern with respectability is today seen as mere hypocrisy. On the contrary, such caution both protected individuals from unnecessarily harsh public censure and maintained the moral image of the community. It is rather the modern love of openness that is a licence for petty cruelty.

Respectability works: it can reduce crime, drunkenness, poverty

Viewed from a utilitarian standpoint (let alone a consideration of individual rights) political correctness is a hideous failure for it has inflicted misery on numerous blameless victims and achieved nothing. Life in the slums of Detroit has not been improved one iota by accusations of racism among academics in Ontario. By contrast respectability works. In the latter half of the 19th century in Britain, Canada, and such American cities as Boston and Philadelphia, the spread of an ethic of respectability brought about improvements in individual conduct that greatly enhanced the quality of life. Crime rates fell so that by the end of the century individuals and their homes were far safer than they are today. Illegitimacy declined, as did the numbers of paupers. Drug addiction and public drunkenness began to decrease. All this was achieved by a spontaneous drive towards respectability on the part of individuals and of voluntary institutions which succeeded in making crime, illegitimacy, pauperism, addiction, and drunkenness appear disreputable in the eyes not only of the middle classes but of the majority of the population.

Today social scientists are apt to sneer at the achievements of that era, to allege that 'middle-class values' were imposed on the lower orders in Britain, to impugn the lack of multi-culturalism in 'Toronto the Good', or to play up the problems caused by Prohibition rather than the gains achieved from the spread of temperance. Yet they are quite unable to provide us with a cure for the social evils of crime, illegitimacy, pauperism, and drug and drink abuse, which have returned on a far greater scale now that the ethic of respectability has been undermined, often by their very efforts.

Respectability's merit: ordinary people can achieve it—you don't have to be successful to be respectable

The great merit of respectability is that it provides a goal in life that is attainable by the vast majority of the population, unlike those two lures of a modern dynamic society, success, which is by definition limited in the number of people who can attain it, and sensation, which is apt to become a limitless thirst. Also the attainment of respectability is a moral achievement in which respect is earned as much by effort as by result. Success, by contrast, though necessary to the proper working of the economy, may well be a question of luck or fashion. Success and respectability are both necessary and complementary goals in a dynamic modern society. If forces such as envy hold able individuals back as has happened in some (though by no means all) Mexican-American communities[1] in the United States, the result is damaging stagnation, a self-defeating cultural defensiveness, and an unjustified resentment of the more go-ahead majority.

Yet at the same time the competition between individuals seeking success has to take place within a moral framework and this is what respectability provides. The honest pharmacist who upholds the standards of the profession and deals fairly with the public, who exhibits the qualities of skill, scrupulous carefulness, and concern for the customer is a respected and respectable person regardless of how successful he or she is. Back-street dealers in illicit drugs are not respectable, however financially successful they may be, precisely because they lack the positive qualities displayed by the pharmacist. The social crisis of our time has arisen because the values of respectability are under-valued relative to the idea of success for its own sake regardless of how it is achieved.[2] What makes the situation worse is the petty excitement associated with a delinquent career, which, in our sensate society (i.e., one that places a high value on immediate sensations), leads it to be preferred over the longer and more arduous process of achievement through the acquisition of skills, judgement, and restraint: the defining characteristics of the respectable man or woman regardless of their degree of financial success.

Respectability ousted by the doctrine of competition and success

The decline of respectability in the 20th century has many complex causes such as secularisation and the increased size of communities or organisations. However, in two respects the collapse of respectability can be linked to the policies and ideologies espoused by politicians of the left and right respectively. On the right, the inappropriate pursuit of efficiency through competition in areas where the market does not operate and, on the left, an obsession with equality, are the sources of our moral decline.

In Britain and America many aspects of life are dominated by an adversarial law system and the tactics of lawyers in areas such as divorce, libel, or accident and negligence claims have lost the legal profession a great deal of the respect it once enjoyed. The pressure to win at all costs has undermined the ethical restraints which are necessary if an adversarial system is to produce fair and honest results. In America the public's cynicism about lawyers has led to a spate of lawyer jokes sufficiently scurrilous to alarm the leaders of the profession:[3]

> 'Why are psychologists using lawyers in their experiments instead of rats?
> The experimenters don't get attached to them and there are some things
> even a rat won't do.'

In a constitutional society based on law, the erosion of respect for a legal profession seen to be losing its respectability is ominous. People in humbler or more peripheral walks of life are less likely to strive to be respectable if they know that such a core institution is in moral crisis. However, even worse problems have arisen in the criminal justice system, first in America and more recently in Britain. Dubious acquittals are common enough in both countries but here I will concentrate on dubious convictions later found to be mistaken. One of the factors that has led to this being a major problem in the United States[4] is the election of district attorneys. All too often, when an incumbent prosecutor needs to seek re-election he will do so on the basis of having a good batting average, i.e., having had convicted and put away a large number of criminals whose depredations on the electors then cease for a time. However, given the pervasiveness of crime, the highly localised organisation of the police, and the innumerable arbitrary rules of procedure and admissibility, it is often difficult to produce a decent quota of spectacular convictions with which to impress the electorate. Under such circumstances the district attorney seeking to keep his job will be strongly tempted to cut corners, conspire with the police to tamper with the evidence, and to conceal facts that would strengthen the case for the defence. The pressure of electoral competition, far from producing a more efficient system of criminal justice, rather tends to corrupt it.

Pursuing successful outcomes at any price subverts respectability especially in the professions

The same may be said of the British police who in the past took a relatively relaxed view of their task because crime in Britain was not a serious social problem. In the period 1950-1970 there were relatively few cases[5] where it could be said with certainty that anyone had been falsely convicted due to the police tampering with the evidence. Since 1970 by contrast there have been a number of cases where people have been convicted of serious crimes and given long jail sentences only for it to be later discovered that the police had concocted crucial parts of the evidence used by the prosecution. There has clearly been a decline in the degree of trustworthiness— a crucial component of respectability—of the British police.

The reason for this lies in part at least in the growing pressure on them to get convictions, particularly in serious cases, as a result of the rising incidence of crime in Britain. Since most criminals who get convicted are either caught in the act or recognised by a member of the public and reported rather than tracked down through proactive detective work, there is not much the police can do to halt the decline in the proportion of crimes that are resolved by the arrest and conviction of the perpetrator. The temptation to cut corners and fix the evidence has thus greatly increased and more individual officers have given way to it. The introduction of performance-related pay for the British police is likely to bring about an even greater wave of corruption in the latter half of the 1990s for, as the temptations increase, professional standards—another key facet of respectability—are likely to collapse.

Already in 1993 the police have massaged the crime figures downwards to produce a spurious fall in the crime rate that is belied by the continued rise in crime shown by the British Crime Survey. If the amount of recorded crime falls, police clear-up rates appear to improve. Another deplorable way of bringing about this illusion is to persuade or induce criminals pleading guilty to one crime to say quite falsely that they were responsible for many other unsolved felonies and misdemeanours. At the best of times, official statistics are problematic but if a new and deliberate bias is added to their imperfections, they will soon become useless not only for the purposes of those who fund the police, but for ordinary citizens who need to know what is going on in their society. There is nothing like accountability for undermining countability, and it is but a short step from fiddling with figures to fiddling with reality and tampering with evidence. There may well be even more false convictions during the next 20 years than there were between 1970 and 1990.

In the law and in teaching

A similar moral may be drawn from the wave of dishonesty among teachers in America following the introduction in the 1980s of multiple choice standardised tests of rudimentary skills in an attempt to measure the teachers' performance and to reward or penalise the individual teachers accordingly. Blatant cheating by supplying students with test answers or altering the answer sheets soon became widespread. A survey in North Carolina showed that over a third of the teachers had either been involved in such cheating or knew of its taking place and major scandals have occurred in Illinois, New Jersey, South Carolina, and Mississippi.[6] Once again an increased pressure for success placed on individuals who could do little to change a system in severe decline resulted in a moral disaster. The teachers, a crucial group in transmitting values of respectability to their pupils, lost their own respectability and respectability lost credibility.

But a deeper threat to respectability has been egalitarianism

On the surface it would appear that the conservative forces in Britain and America were entirely to blame for those fiascos. It was they, after all, whose crude use of measuring devices and incentives led to the demoralisation in both senses of the police and the teachers. The real responsibility, however, lies on the left, for it is their all-pervasive egalitarianism that has made the tasks of police and teachers alike an impossible one. They no longer have the authority that they need to carry out their tasks effectively; it has been taken away from them by educational administrators with a philosophy of education that is child-centred not learning-centred and by constitutional lawyers more concerned to protect criminals than their victims. A common thread of 'under-doggery' runs through both situations and the result is a failure properly to address the questions 'What does a teacher do when faced with pupils who do not want to learn and are often disrupters of the learning of others?' and 'What can a police officer achieve in an area where there is no respect for law and order?'. The teachers and the police who have to operate the system have been made scapegoats for the deficiencies of those who designed and constrained it, much as factory directors or store managers in the old centrally-planned Soviet Union were blamed for the idiocies of the planners.

The failure of radical conservative planning

The collapse of respectability among a substantial section of the most crucial guardians of respectability is an indication of a very real problem. How under such circumstances can schools act as agents for instilling respectability into pupils as they did in the past? In part the answer has to lie in an attempt to *recreate* that orderly past, with a corresponding abandonment of the conservative mood of macho-radicalism that has sought to squeeze extra productivity out of institutions by external bureaucratic pressure. So long as these institutions remain committed to unattainable and undesirable egalitarian ends, efforts to make them productive are bound to fail because the two sets of aims are utterly contradictory. The only form of equality that should be aimed at is the equality of the respectable, i.e., of those who deserve respect for their personal qualities. One advantage at least of striving to recover an aspect of the past, in this case respectability, is that we do have some idea of what the past was like and of how to operate its institutions. As such it is a better basis for policy than the mad bursts of 'rational' planning, complete with a farrago of mission statements, aims, and objectives, that conservative radicals have taken over from the defunct sloganising socialism of Eastern Europe.

Approbation to children is what respectability is to adults—a workable incentive

If schools are to become bastions of respectability once more, one of the key elements that must be re-incorporated into education and particularly the education of the very youngest children, is approbation. Approbation is for children what respectability is for adults—a means of attaching them to virtue through the positive opinions of others. Honesty, diligence, self-control, kindness, and a sense of duty and obligation are all virtues that can be acquired by the vast majority of children. Because they are praiseworthy virtues, the children who exhibit them are worthy of praise and this should be used as a means of encouraging virtue from their earliest years. At present adults are strangely reluctant to use approbation in this way lest those children who have been greatly praised should become smug and feel themselves to be morally superior to their unpraised and, possibly in consequence, jealous contemporaries. Thus equality is standing in the way of the promotion and reward of virtue. On the contrary, we should polish juvenile halos and hug the smug. Better smugger today than mugger tomorrow.

Adult approbation of children versus delinquent peer pressure. Fairness as the solvent of morality

Virtuous or improving children should be selectively showered with approbation long before they are able to understand the meaning of the virtues that constitute respectability or can comprehend why they are necessary. For young children it may well be futile to try and spell out the reasons for a particular rule; it is enough to make it clear that 'this is the way we do things here; people like us don't do that" and to appeal to the child's wish to conform to the traditions and customs of the group. For most children the alternative to conforming to the moral standards imposed on them by adults is not moral autonomy but conformity to the social pressure of their (often delinquent) peers. The influence of children of the same age and of older children is not, as progressive psychologists have suggested, a source of patterns of constructive co-operation that enable the child to become a mature moral agent, but a dangerous force when outside adult control. Potential delinquents and deviants become more delinquent and deviant in order to tap an alternative source of approbation—that of slightly older and bolder delinquents and deviants. The only way to prevent this is to isolate younger children as far as possible from the undesirable influence of older ones and to ensure that adults have a monopoly of the power to confer approbation and approval as well as blame and shame.

It is particularly important *not* to try and justify the rules by reducing them to some crude model of fairness. To do so is to provide children with a set of excuses that they can use to neutralise the very restraints that we are trying to build into each child's conscience: 'It is unfair that Tommy has two apples so I shall steal one of them', 'It is unfair that teacher gave me a bad mark, so I shall yandalise her motor-bike', 'It is unfair that Patty has naturally curly hair, so I shall pull it out by the roots'. Fairness is not the source but the solvent of morality, the insidious means by which necessary social rules are questioned, relativised, and undermined. If moral rules can always be challenged in the name of fairness, then delinquency will be rife among those who would otherwise have conformed to the ordinary moral rules of society.

Respectability and approbation are both tried and tested techniques for attaching people to virtue which have become unpopular in a society that is obsessed with equality and governed in an increasingly bureaucratic way. There is no reason why they should not be used successfully today as they were a century ago. They may today be contrary to the spirit of our times, but then it is that same spirit of our time that is responsible for our current state of moral disorder.

CHAPTER 9

The Necessity and Desirability of Being Repressed:

Freudianism, Behaviourism, and the Denial of Human Agency

Joseph F. Rychlak

Those who exhibit self-restraint today are called repressed by some psychologists

There are two major interpretations of *repression* in vogue today, both of which seek to offset or rectify the negatives of such a psychological state through positive efforts. The first, 'inner' interpretation derives from a certain understanding of psychoanalysis. The suggestion here is that it is bad to be repressed, and that ideally the person should release pent-up inhibitions whenever possible. A person who values self-control over impulsiveness is pictured as being uptight, suffering a hang-up, or defensively fearing to 'let go' in spontaneous gratification of whatever it is that has brought the repression about. This attitude toward personal restraint implies a specific therapeutic approach. Thus, the person with a neurosis is believed to be suffering from a repressed dynamic that occurred in early childhood and now intrudes on successful adjustment as if it were an infected (psychic) boil. Once freed from this dynamic, a suitable adjustment is made possible. The release afforded from this inner repression is what supposedly effects the cure, of the order of lancing a distending infection.

Others mean by repression that humans are conditioned by their environment

Our second interpretation is a kind of 'outer' repression that has been advanced by non-analytical behaviourist psychologists. This repression is said to be due to adverse environmental manipulations of one sort or another, injuring the person who has no psychic resources available to counter such influences. Key descriptive terms and phrases in this context would include negatively conditioned, aversively shaped, punished, frustrated, and so on. The repression suffered may be traced to past negative social circumstances that have left their mark on the person, or are said to exist in the present cultural milieu. In either case, it follows that if a therapeutic outcome is to be achieved, these negatives must be offset by the application of suitable positives. To hold the person responsible is tantamount to 'blaming the victim'. To expect self-improvement is unrealistic given the power of the repressing environment to influence the individual. If it cannot be avoided altogether, any form of punishment is to be used sparingly and only as a last resort. To apply further negatives is to heap coals on a roaring fire.

Both interpretations disapprove of reprimand and both deny the power of individuals to choose and take responsibility

Although it is not clear on first consideration, what both of these interpretations have in common is that they are based on an image of humanity that is non-agential. An agent is an organism that can influence its behaviour, that has a 'free will' to behave in conformity with or in opposition to prompting influences from the social or physical environment. Agency is a concept in need of discussion these days, where we find ourselves greatly concerned over the steady decline in the respect shown to morality. If there is no such thing as human agency then there can be no such thing as individual responsibility, personal honesty, or commitment to a moral code.

I would like to explain how our two interpretations of repression have come about, show why they are unable to address the core issues of human agency, and then propose an alternative image of humanity that is more suitable to the task which lies ahead—which is to revitalize the sagging values of concern and respect for others. Before we can find a sense of common humanity we must first know what humanity means in our own personhood.

The two interpretations came from a common source: a restricted view of what science can say about human actions

Our two interpretations of repression take basic root from the same source—a Newtonian restriction on the kind of causes one is permitted to use to explain anything in physical reality. For some 2,000 years, philosophers, theologians, and then scientists have grounded their explanations in terms of Aristotle's *four* causal meanings.[1] The Greek word Aristotle used for cause was *aitía*, which has the meaning of *responsibility*, so that in following his usage we would be trying to assign responsibility for why something existed or an event took place. The names for the causes were coined by Aristotle, but all four meanings had been employed previously by other philosophers. We can treat these meanings as four explanatory predications.

Aristotle's explanation of cause: efficient, material, and formal causes

Thus, to explain anything in experience we can use one or more of the following predicates. First, we can use a *material cause*, in which case we are trying to account for something based on what kind of substance 'makes it up'; for example, making a chair out of wood results in an item with different properties and a shorter 'life' expectancy than one made of marble. Second, we can use an *efficient cause*, in which case we would try to capture the impetus, push, or thrust in events that go to assemble them, or to cue them along as they unfold; billiard balls bumping each other about on a cushioned table or flashing red lights of emergency vehicles in traffic exemplify such causation. Third, we could also bring a *formal cause* meaning to bear, in which case we would be using the essential pattern, shape, or order of events or objects as a basis for descriptive understanding; thus, the patterned sequence of a mathematical proof or the shape of a friend's physiognomy enable us to know something about what is taking place as we sit in the mathematics class or spy a friendly face in the crowd.

And final cause: cause as purpose

We can also use the *final cause* or, as Aristotle called it, 'that for the sake of which' an action takes place or anything is said to *be* in existence; final causes subsume the meaning of reason, purpose, or intention. The reason a person has a yearly physical is *for the sake of* maintaining a satisfactory level of health.

Final causes deal with ends, and as the Greek word for end is *telos*, we refer to explanations relying on final causation as teleologies or telic accounts. Teleological explanation was common in science until the 16th century when a combination of historical occurrences was to 'do in' such theoretical explanations. Galileo's notorious clash with the churchmen of the Inquisition was one major source of the decline in teleological description among scientists. The churchmen, relying on Biblical accounts of God's intentions in His creations, had the solar system *geocentric*, whereas Galileo was proposing a Copernican *heliocentric* explanation of the solar system and offered empirical evidence in support of his view. Galileo's empirical views therefore countered the recorded 'divine intentions' of a deity. His house arrest and recantation heralded the beginning of the demise of final-cause description in science. A deity teleology is not the same thing as a human teleology, but the very idea of assigning intentions to scientific explanations was brought into question by this confrontation between science and religion.

Over use of cause as purpose led to criticism and decline

Another major source of the decline in telic explanation stemmed from what might be termed the Aristotelian excesses in use of the causes. Aristotle favoured using all four of the causal meanings in *every* scientific explanation, believing that this could only enrich the account. He attributed purposivity to everything in nature, suggesting that leaves exist *for the sake of* providing shade for the fruit on trees.[2] It was Sir Francis Bacon who led the assault on such final-cause ascriptions to inanimate events. Pointing his guns at Aristotle, Bacon said that it is bad scientific explanation to suggest that leaves on trees are *for the sake of* shading fruit, or that bones are *for the sake of* holding up the fleshy parts of the body.[3] Bacon asked what it added to our understanding of trees or physical bodies to make such attributions. Since we can explain physical structures and events completely using material and efficient causation, we should confine our scientific accounts to these predications. Even formal-cause patterns in nature (e.g., the funnel cloud of a tornado) are made up of some combination of material and efficient causations (e.g., wind pressure and debris). Bacon criticized over-reliance on formal causation as a 'basic' explanation.[4] He did not reject formal and final causation altogether, feeling that such conceptions were proper in the realm of human affairs such as metaphysics and ethics.

Cause as purpose highly relevant to decision-making yet ruled out by Newtonian science

This allusion to the more abstract realms of metaphysics and especially ethics should catch our attention because this is what we are concerned with here. Ethical decisions cannot really be framed in material- and efficient-cause terms. Indeed, decision-making *per se* cannot be extracted from material- and efficient-cause predications. We are now in the realm of some patterned belief system, an evaluation, a comparative judgement rendered in the light of certain grounding assumptions or convictions. Only the meanings of formal and final causation can subsume such explanations.

The first wave of what was then called 'modern' science issuing in the 17th century was Newtonian. The emphasis in Newtonian science was to rely exclusively on material- and efficient-cause explanations. Indeed, the phrase 'natural science' is tantamount to saying 'science without final causation'. This is important to our present task, for both Freudian psychoanalysis and behaviourist psychology were nurtured in the Newtonian limitation on causal description.

Sigmund Freud's concept of repression: a biological or psychological theory? Is there room for will and responsibility?

Although he was in my opinion fundamentally teleological in his view of the person,[5] Freud was forced by his colleagues to convey his thoughts on abnormal behaviour in terms of the medical model—which is a variant form of Newtonianism. The upshot is that there are always two ways in which to understand a Freudian dynamic—one that is purely psychological and the other that is expressed in a quasi-physical sense. To accomplish this latter form of explanation, Freud resorted to his notoriously awkward libido theory. Although it has the intimation of a physical energy, libido is purely psychic. It supposedly energizes the mind, but cannot be captured or measured in any way. Neither is libido that 'good feeling' (pleasure) that one experiences when indulging in a positive experience (e.g., sexual orgasm). But libido is supposedly involved in repression.

Thus, a portion of the personality structure (e.g., the Censor or the Ego) can employ libido to repress or 'block' unacceptable wishes being sent forward from unconsciousness to consciousness by a different portion of the personality (e.g., the Id). When this checkmate occurs at a totally unconscious level we speak of repression; and when it occurs at a more conscious level of mind we speak of suppression.[6] We might repress a lustful desire for our parent due to its revolting nature, but merely suppress a desire to 'peek' into a public lavatory used by the opposite sex. The reason that repression occurs so readily at the unconscious level is because in the unconscious 'no process that resembles "judging" occurs'.[7] The unconscious does not condemn an idea because it is morally reprehensible. It is consciousness that renders such teleological evaluations of the meaning that ideas entertain. The unconscious is amoral.

Freud had been speculating on the possibility that one idea could block another since the early 1890s. This was before he had introduced the libido theory. In 1892 he advanced his first real theory of neurosis in which he spoke of antithetical ideas and a counter-will functioning in the personality, leading a female patient to block her intention and enact its very opposite.[8]

107

She told herself to be quiet while attending to her sleeping infant only to clack her tongue loudly. Anything like repression at this point in Freud's theorizing was strictly psychological—the meaning of one idea opposing another. But after he had been pressured by colleagues into giving his theory a more medico-biological emphasis with the libido theory, we find Freud for the first time in 1907 using the phrase 'repression of an instinctual impulse'.[9] This emphasis is more biological than psychological, and it suggests that the impulse rather than the meaning surrounding this (presumably physical) impulse is what results in abnormality.

At this point we see a greater emphasis on the role of consciousness in the repressive process,[10] but the unconscious is always involved. Freud worked the concept of repression into his developmental theory, suggesting that 'fixations' occurred which continually re-enacted unresolved problems that arose during certain maturational stages in life.[11] He then began speaking of fixations as involving 'dammed-up libido' and this in turn facilitated the further shift to a belief that psychoanalytical cure involves the release of pent-up energies *per se*. Today, it is not uncommon to hear that a cure in psychoanalysis involves the 'release of the repressed', but something very fundamental is being overlooked here, namely: the meaning of the repressed mental content that is released.

Will, consideration, and intention cannot be banished entirely from Freudian repression

For example, Freud once referred to a male patient who had had a repressed (unconscious) death wish against his brother-in-law.[12] This repressed wish 'had been made conscious during the treatment the year before and the consequences which had followed from its repression had yielded to treatment. But it still persisted, and though it was no longer pathogenic, it was sufficiently intense. It might be described [at present] as a "suppressed" wish'.[13] Freud here tells us that the repressed idea of wishing for another person's death was brought into awareness and analyzed, but it still did not 'go away'. And surely the ethico-moral implications of such an act did not 'go away'. So, two points may be made clear here: first, relieving the patient of a repression does not effect an automatic release from the content of what has been repressed; and, second, the content of what has been repressed (unconsciously) may demand that it be suppressed (consciously) in the ongoing life of the patient.

Freud also noted that there is always a risk in the uncovering of neurotic dynamics, because we strip the patient of a defence and force him or her to confront thoughts that to date have been avoided (albeit at a price!). He then added 'The unhappiness that our work of enlightenment may cause will after all only affect some individuals. The change-over to a more realistic and creditable attitude on the part of society will not be bought too dearly by these sacrifices'.[14] We might conclude from this statement that Freud embraced a certain degree of social revisionism in his theory. But surely it cannot be suggested that the removing of repression is all that there is to dealing with neuroses. Repressed material brought to consciousness must be dealt with, and invariably this amounts to a struggle over some issue, which is the reason why repression occurred in the first place. And although technically speaking, we do not repress 'at will', we can do something of the sort in suppressing ideas that prompt us to behave in certain ways rather than others. At least we can do so if in fact we are agents, with the capacity to judge our behaviour on certain (moral) grounds and behave for the sake of the meanings extending from these grounds. Before turning to this possibility, we will look briefly at our other form of repression.

Second understanding of repression—behaviourism—banishes will and understanding. Man as machine

Newtonian science had an even greater influence on academic psychology than it did on Freudian psychoanalysis. Freud made an effort to conform to Newtonian injunctions even as he tried to capture the telic side of behaviour. As we have seen, his libido theory was such a concession to the reductive efforts being made in natural science to explain objects and events by reducing them to the underlying material/efficient causes (energies) that presumably moulded them and moved them along. But in the academic circles of Europe and then America, another approach was being worked out in which an even more direct form of Newtonian reductionism was embraced. I refer here to the mechanistic formulations of behaviourism. John B. Watson, the oft-cited father of behaviourism, summed things up perfectly when he said '*Let us try to think of man as an assembled organic machine ready to run*'.[15] A machine or any form of mechanical explanation is captured exclusively through material and especially efficient causation; there is *no* final cause meaning involved here at all.[16]

If we believe that people are machines then they are no longer agents. They cannot evaluate and then set the grounds for the sake of which they will be influenced, determined, shaped, and so forth. This has been the guiding assumption of behaviourist theory for most of the 20th century. Rather than look to the individual for a personal influence on behaviour, we must look to the environment, because all the person can do is respond in efficient-cause fashion to the stimulations of the environment. This image of humanity is what moved B. F. Skinner, another famous behaviourist, to say that 'men will never become originating centers of control, because their behavior will itself be controlled, but their role as mediators may be extended without limit'.[17] Mediating mechanisms are not capable of rendering judgements. A mediator simply takes in predetermined influences and moves them along as indicated without the capacity to contradict or negate what is already under way.

In drawing out the specific manner in which a machine-like person was to be shaped by environmental forces of an efficient-cause nature, the behaviourists worked out their theory of behavioral reinforcement. The person, as any animal in nature, responds more reliably and consistently if behaviour is shaped through positive reinforcements. This can occur through satisfying a drive state, as when we are relieved of hunger through eating. Or, just any kind of contingent circumstance following an action of ours that is empirically seen to increase our behaviour in one way rather than another is said to be positively reinforcing. The child who laughingly continues running through a lawn sprinkler on a hot day is being positively reinforced— or this behaviour would *not* be repeated.

Although it is possible to effect changes through a negative or an aversive reinforcement, this kind of manipulation is sometimes unreliable and generally frowned upon by the behaviourists. The behaviourist always aims at a positively reinforcing rather than a negatively reinforcing form of manipulation. So any therapeutic effort would involve applying positive reinforcements to desired behaviour, and ignoring—hence extinguishing—the stimulations that trigger the maladaptive behaviour. At no point in this programme of manipulation is there any assumption being made that the person under such control is capable of contradicting or negating what is taking place. The only way a person can contradict an influence is if he or she has been previously shaped to do so. As a mediating mechanism, there is no process available to the person enabling an evaluation of the 'that for the sake of which' variety to be made.

Man as computer

In recent years, a so-called cognitive revolution is said to have taken place in psychology.[18] What this amounts to is moving from Watson's machine metaphor, which was probably something like an automobile, to the metaphor of an electronic computer. However, we still have a machine

110

under direction, with no teleology involved. The reinforcement concept is not important to computer modelling, which relies on a 'software' programme to direct the actions of the 'hardware' machine process. The various schemata employed by the programme are presumably learned through experience, acting therefore as a kind of mediator, but the precise way in which this learning takes place is rarely made explicit.[19] A typical explanation relies on frequency, suggesting that a computing intelligence will somehow retain what it frequently encounters as relevant to the directing programme.[20] Once again, of course, there is no true decision-making or selection taking place here.

The combined effect of our two interpretations of repression is to weaken the traditionally valued behavioral patterns known variously as will, strength of character, self-denial, and personal restraint. Human behaviour has been cast on the receiving end of influences stemming from the biological or social realm. There are no technical terms in current psychological circles to describe how an agent might, in fact, assertively contradict or negate promptings from the bio-physical or environmental realm in a truly 'free' manner. This is a serious weakness in psychological explanation, one that needs to be corrected.

Back to the final cause: the recognition of will, understanding, purpose, and responsibility. Oppositionality fundamental

I believe that to recast human behaviour in agential terms we must return to final-cause description. It is the agent who evaluates the previously repressed contents, takes up the reasons why repression was attempted in the first place, and then works to rectify the circumstances involved—including an intentional suppression of many 'impulses' still hanging about as 'possibilities for acting' in the psychic realm. It is the agent who, although routinely conforming to social pressures, occasionally evaluates what is taking place and decides whether to continue in this routine manner based on some personally affirmed slate of values (beliefs, moral principles, universals, etc.). Agents can act in conformity with, in opposition to, or without regard for the many physical or social promptings of life. This capacity is what is popularly referred to as 'free will'.

But how is such agency possible? It can only be understood by returning to the final-cause description of human behaviour that psychology has been intentionally avoiding for over a century. I believe that Freud actually wanted to embrace the telic image of the person, but compromised with the Newtonians of his time by cleverly hiding this non-mechanistic formulation under a cloud of pseudo-mechanism (libido theory). Teleology does not damage the essence of Freudian theory, but it does have a detrimental impact on behaviourism's mechanistic formulations. Regardless, I think that not only empirical findings,[21] but also recent history in human relations are establishing with certainty that people are not organic machines 'ready to run'.[22] Nor are they organic computers 'ready to calculate' whatever is entered into them without the capacity to evaluate and modify the meanings so 'input'.[23]

I think that from the very outset of life, people are organisms who are *ready to predicate* experience. They do not merely respond in efficient-cause fashion to antecedent influences as the behaviourists would have it. Human beings take positions in life, they affirm a patterned belief (formal cause) 'for the sake of which' (final cause) they behave. I call this process a *telosponse*. To telospond is to affirm a predicating meaning which acts as a context to be extended into ongoing experience. We do not leave a room by 'responding' to the stimulation of the door before us. We leave a room by affirming the formal-cause pattern of the room as we construe it, in which the door is located where we presume it to be, and then we behave for the sake of this predication.

There is something quite distinctive about predication in telosponsivity. I can point this out most directly by relying on Euler circles, as used in logical analysis. If I contend that 'John is reliable' we can symbolize my assertion by using two circles—one large, one small. The small circle symbolizes 'John' and the large circle symbolizes 'reliability' or 'reliable people'. We then place the larger over the smaller circle. The meaning of this larger, context-providing circle immediately frames the smaller circle, extending the meaning of reliability to John. This is how I am contending that people 'work' cognitively. People frame targets (like John) with meanings that frame and extend to them (reliability 'to' John). There is always a broader range of meaning in the predicating than in the targeted circle (i.e., others besides John are also reliable, there are many different ways in which to manifest reliability, etc.).

Moreover, note that there is both an inside and an outside to the predicating (larger) circle. This inside-outside symbolizes an *oppositionality* in the process of human reason that does not exist in a machine process. As human beings we constantly face alternatives by way of opposite implications in all that we do. Indeed, oppositionality is fundamental to judgement and choice. Humans reflect this oppositional reasoning when they contradict beliefs, or negate them, or contrast them in some way (e.g., is John *real-*

ly reliable? How do we know? On what grounds can we conclude this?).
Humans are not simply mediators of inputs and outputs. A machine takes
an input 'as is' and never questions it so long as it meets the design or pro-
grammed procedure called for. A human being always senses what the input
'is not', grasps a direction that is contrary to the input, and hence is psy-
chologically called upon to 'take a position' on the bipolarities of meaning
that life continually engenders. This is why the person matters. This is why
agency exists.

Once we admit purpose, repression emerges as potentially necessary and desirable, an act of self-control

Agency is the result of a predicating intelligence framed within a sea of
oppositionality. Freudian repression is of this nature, as reflected in the anti-
thetic idea concept. One idea intentionally blocks another based on some
reason (a 'that' for the sake of which the conflict occurs). When this reason
is not consciously admitted, the oppositionality is termed repression. When
the reason is known consciously, the oppositionality is termed suppression.
It is up to the agent to decide on the grounds for the sake of which his or
her behaviour will follow. Agents take responsibility for these decisions, and
therefore they must occasionally take criticism or experience failure when
things do not work out as projected. Life is not one long series of positive
reinforcements. What we call 'character' is germinated in the graceful
acceptance of life's negative reinforcements, as well as overcoming them
through personal effort. Agents also reap the benefits of praise and satisfaction when decisions are successful. Finally, agents know that for an orderly
and satisfying personal life, as well as promoting tranquillity in social affairs,
a degree of self-suppression (conscious 'repression') is not only inevitable
but highly desirable.

CHAPTER 10

Trust:

Lessons from the Military in the Reconstruction of Civic Culture

Christopher Dandeker

The disintegration of traditional institutions

The last 15 years have seen the attempt to run and evaluate traditional institutions, parliament, the professions, the financial institutions, the church, the monarchy, national life itself, on a meritocratic model. It is an approach which involves the search for and measurement of the outcomes of institutions, and often in the short term. The same period has been one of decline and growing public disenchantment with these institutions and there is a renewed interest in other ways of running and evaluating them, ways which recognise the integrating role of virtues in traditional institutional life: honour, lifetime service, character, trust.

In seeking to reunderstand how these virtues work in sustaining institutions, the military is an instructive case to consider. For it is the home *par excellence* of such virtues; but it too has suffered disintegration through the misapplication of foreign standards; and it is in a special position to teach society, standing as it does, as the very basis of social order.

The extent of the disintegration

Martin Jacques has argued that 'Faith in our legal system has been shaken by a series of miscarriages of justice. The police are no longer viewed as paragons of virtue. Our civil service is not held in anything like the esteem it once was. Parliament, like politicians, has lost the respect it used to command. The disestablishment of the church is being seriously debated. The honours system, notwithstanding cosmetic attempts at reform, is widely discredited'.[1]

Indeed, the future of the monarchy is now debated quite seriously (including in some military circles—at least informally) in full recognition that, in

117

doing so, one raises the question of larger constitutional and institutional reform. As Jacques admits, and the opinion polls confirm, at least until the recent furore over the peccadilloes of the Chief of the Defence Staff, who resigned, it appears that only the armed forces are still held in high regard and their professionalism respected.[2] This has all been too much for the political commentator, Stephen Glover, who feels '. . . sick to see the world of my youth coming apart before my very eyes . . .'.[3]

This disintegration can be partially explained by particular facts such as the longevity of the Conservative Government. But more basic reasons are the misapplication of classical liberalism—'market forces'—to non-market institutions, the end of the Cold War, and the increasing intrusion of a debunking media.

Forces for disintegration: the 1960s critique of authority and 1980s meritocracy

The contemporary media have benefited, ironically, from a confluence of two cultural trends: the 1960's critique of all forms of authority and the 1980's spirit of meritocracy. While the first institutionalized irreverence as a cultural style, the second not only defined achievement narrowly in monetary terms, it also encouraged the, by no means unrealistic, belief that upward social mobility did not require acceptance of the traditional social and moral values of those long-established members of the middle and upper-middle classes. A small but significant example of this was Harry Enfield's caricature 'loadsamoney'. Much to its creator's chagrin, what started out as a political critique of what he considered to be a distasteful social trend ended up being imitated and celebrated by the very 'arriviste' people it was meant to challenge. (Apparently this was why Mr. Enfield killed off the character.) It should be stressed that 'loadsamoney' characters in the 1980s could be found in prosperous sectors of working *and* so called 'yuppie' middle classes, especially in the fast expanding financial services sector. (Their influence spread a good deal further in that decade.)

In any event, upward social mobility has added to the trend towards irreverence—all institutions now have within them individuals with the skills appropriate for their jobs but increasingly questioning about the moral landscape of their occupations. Socially and culturally, Britain is now not so much a divided society but a fragmented one with a diversity of moral and other viewpoints each keen to assert its 'rights', not least that it be deferred to so long as deference is not asked of it. In such a fragmented environment, an already shaky traditional order is hardly likely to flourish.

Disintegration—a trend recognized in the 19th century

Is all this uncertainty and anguish about the breakdown of community by unfettered market forces really new? The corrosive power of market principles when applied to traditional institutions was a significant talking point for much of the 19th century, not least in the 1840s. Here is Karl Marx talking, famously, and ambivalently about the dynamism of modern capitalism:

> The bourgeoisie, wherever it has got the upper hand, has put an end to all feudal, patriarchal, idyllic relations. It has pitilessly torn asunder the motley feudal ties that bound man to his "natural superiors", and has left remaining no other nexus between man and man than naked self interest, than callous "cash payment". It has drowned the most heavenly ecstasies of religious fervour, of chivalrous enthusiasm, of Philistine sentimentalism in the icy water of egotistical calculation . . . Constant revolutionising of production, uninterrupted disturbance of all social conditions, everlasting uncertainty and agitation distinguish the bourgeois epoch from all earlier ones. All fixed, fast-frozen relations, with their train of ancient and venerable prejudices and opinions, are swept away, all new ones become antiquated before they can ossify. All that is solid melts into air, all that is holy is profaned and man is at last compelled to face with sober senses his real conditions of life and his relations with his kind.[5]

Since at least the early 19th century, therefore, there have been periodic cries of anguish about 'the world we have lost' and, in consequence, attempts to reconstruct the moral and social basis of a community in the conditions of industrial society. Yet, there *is* something new about the current crisis (a crisis which, leaving aside some national idiosyncrasies, can be found in other modern societies in Europe and North America). In what can be called these 'new times' a common thread is uncertainty and anxiety.[6]

The end of the Cold War and the new climate of uncertainty

The first and most obvious feature of these 'New Times' is the immediate effect of the end of the Cold War on the international order of states. The certainties of the bi-polar standoff between the two superpowers have given way to a more uncertain multipolar world. In this uncertain and turbulent world it is more difficult than ever before to identify where one's international interests lie and thus what appropriate mix of military and non-military (economic, diplomatic) instruments of security should be developed.

Secondly, we now live in a globally integrated economy created by the electronic revolution in the means of communication, to which companies, states, and other organizations have to adjust.[7] Modern means of transport and communication facilitate the rapid spread of cultural and other products from one society to another, including the movement of populations: for example, the impact of television images of the West on the revolt

119

against Communism in the 1980s in Eastern Europe and on migratory movements today in the east and south of the European Community.[8]

Globalisation has not only integrated the world economy to a greater degree than before; it has also made different regions of societies susceptible to the security consequences of shifts of capital, raw materials, and population from one part of the world to another, as for instance in the global sourcing of modern manufacturing products such as automobiles and computers.[9] The cycle of good and bad times is increasingly dependent upon transnational processes. Populations of all states—including their leaders and advisors—have to come to terms with the paradox that global unification and fragmentation are mutually reinforcing.

The modern state in the new global order

Thirdly, globalisation and regionalisation have led to two quite different political developments. On the one hand, there has been what Kennedy and other writers have referred to as the relocation of political authority to supra-national political agencies such as the European Community on the regional level and the UN, other international organizations, and the transnational corporation at the global level.[10] On the other hand, there has been a contrary development: the relocation of authority to regionalist and/or separatist and sub-national movements and agencies within the nation-state, even amongst what observers have regarded as the more mature examples in Western Europe.[11]

Both of these developments can be viewed as responses to globalisation and regionalisation and thus as deep-rooted challenges to the traditional nation-state from both above and below. Sub-national conflicts are, therefore, not simply to be regarded as effects of the 'unfreezing' of ethnic and national rivalries made possible by the end of the Cold War, but as responses to the impact of the global economy on relations between core and peripheral regions of societies and attempts by regions to obtain better terms from their nation state and/or the supra-national agencies that have emerged in recent decades. This climate of turbulence within and between nation states is exacerbated by a relative shift of the economic centres of world capitalism from the U.S. and Europe to the dynamic Pacific economies.

From a military point of view, sub-national tensions are likely to pose serious difficulties for the advanced societies. Some Western states have shown themselves to be vulnerable to regional/separatist political problems and conflicts as is evident from events in Northern Ireland, Spain, Canada, and Italy. Potentially more violent fissures are apparent in Central and Eastern Europe. Many of these conflicts cut across existing political boundaries and even in the case of more straightforward civil wars, the industrial democracies are likely to be drawn, willingly or not, into various forms of peace-keeping and peacemaking.[12] Here again, circumstances are rather different from before. To be sure, there is nothing especially peculiar about a multi-polar international state system—regional and world politics have experienced cycles moving from uni-, multi-, and bi-polar systems in different historical periods. What is new is the coincidence of the structural principles of multipolarity and multicentric orders. A plethora of 'sovereignty-free' state actors—NGOs, corporations, parties, media organizations, and so on—now play a role in international politics. They complicate the environment in which states operate both in regard to their external and their internal affairs. These organizations can achieve a global presence and ensure that the space of international politics is no longer the exclusive preserve of the state. To this extent the assumptions of political realism have to be rethought. States now have the difficult task of designing a legal and normative basis for a multipolar and multicentric order; and in doing so they have to weigh up the relative value of military and non-military instruments in securing that order.

For all these reasons there is something new about the predicament faced by those seeking to confront the problems of moral order in contemporary industrial society. The modern nation-state is implicated in a dynamic, often bewildering set of global processes of change. These have to be taken into account when considering some of the problems of particular countries, as will be shown below with regard to Britain.

The new search for community

Whatever the successes achieved by the application of market principles to British institutions—and these have been considerable in terms of productivity in business and public sector organizations—a key weakness in the Thatcherite agenda has been a failure to develop fully enough the moral dimension of market society—a society based on individual freedom and moral responsibility for self and others. The path from 'Victorian Values' to 'Back to Basics' has hardly been a successful one. The latter in particular was regarded by many as an unrealistic and fogeyish attempt to turn the clock back and in any case it swiftly became a farce and simply a means of revealing the hypocrisy of some of its defenders in public life. However, the attempt to build a society based not just on market exchange but a moral framework of personal responsibility and obligations rooted in civic virtues was admirable in its overall identification of the problem but faulty in identifying the means necessary to resolve it. This was because, deep down, the Thatcherite agenda is as utilitarian on moral issues as its socialist counterpart.

At the same time the weakness of socialism is twofold: first its failure to think clearly about individuals rather than collectivities such as class. Now that Marxism is discredited, class has been upstaged by special interest groups in regard to which the political task is to build 'rainbow coalitions'. Secondly, there is a tendency to think that moral questions are actually all about the effective supply of enough goods and services to meet some criterion of an acceptable economic standard of living.

In the space or moral vacuum created by the conflict between socialist collectivism and conservative market individualism, attempts are being made to engineer a way through the current moral crisis, as, for example, current debates on how to reconstruct community to meet the social and moral requirements of the 21st century. Recently, discussions of citizenship have, quite properly, begun to shift away from an exclusive focus on the rights of individuals to a consideration of the appropriate balance between rights and duties—or obligations. This has involved a political recovery of the importance of 'civic culture' in providing a basis for the moral order of modern society through a critique of the inadequacies of Marxist collectivism on the one hand and liberal market economics on the other. Neither of these philosophies provide a proper space for civic culture—a system whereby individuals are attached to each other through a network of moral obligations: Marxism obliterates the responsible individual with rights and obligations by subsuming him into a set of needs and rights that are provided by the collectivist structures of the bureaucratic state. Free market economics, on the other hand, focuses on individuals as self-seeking, economically motivated egos with little attachment to a moral order of civic obligations: the space of civic culture is occupied by the cash nexus and satisfaction of economic wants. The key political and philosophical challenge today is to provide an analysis of the conditions under which a civic order can be created to fit the conditions of modern society.

New proposals for community vitiated by utilitarians

Much of the left's recent interest in the concept of community reveals its deep-rooted utilitarianism. Consider the following comments from one of the more thoughtful and perceptive writers, Martin Jacques. For him, the key values for Britain's 'elites and governing institutions' as we prepare for the next century are

> Porousness and openness; meritocracy, social diversity, a plurality of skills, and youth, professionalism, efficiency, application and success, transparency and accountability; vision, change, strategy and a sense of the future; flat hierarchies, networking and leadership; innovation, experimentation, radicalism, cosmopolitanism and eclecticism.[13]

Revealingly, Jacques continues, 'Many of these values have already taken root in parts of our society, including our best companies'.

Social cohesion (and economic survival in a globalised world system) should, it would appear, rest upon society being modelled like a successful business. But what would be the moral basis of this meritocratic hierarchy in which social relations are organized in terms of the free exchange of expertise? For the fast moving fragmented world which Jacques seeks to restore to some sort of order, a restatement of markets and a belief in openness and all ideas open to challenge is pretty small beer. How would such a moral outlook prevent the drift to a new tribalism that appears to be the trend in the U.S. today, where Jacques appears to be looking for inspiration? When one considers what is absent from his list of virtues it is plain to see that his stated solution is actually part of the problem: tradition, loyalty, honesty, integrity, honour, steadfastness, service, self-sacrifice, self-respect, duty or obligation, and trust.

The need for deeper ties

As I have argued elsewhere, Durkheim has provided one of the most eloquent rebuttals of the moral poverty of a society based on exchange and technical expertise:

> (E)ven where society relies most completely upon the division of labour, it does not become a jumble of juxtaposed atoms, between which it can establish only external transient contacts. Rather the members are united by ties which extend deeper and far beyond the short moments during which the exchange is made . . .[14]

He continues,

> (A)ltruism is not destined to become . . . a sort of agreeable ornament to social life but *it will forever be its fundamental basis.* How can we ever really dispense with it? Men cannot live together without acknowledging and, consequently making

mutual sacrifices, without tying themselves to one another with strong, durable bonds. Every society is a moral society. [emphasis added]15

In addressing the task of reconstructing the moral basis of community it is critical to avoid 'knee jerk' old-fogeyism or 'back to basics' and to ask what specific traditions are of continuing relevance to today's conditions. For example, as I have argued elsewhere, national service schemes could not succeed without building in the idea of alternatives to military service.[16] This point raises the wider question of the relevance of traditional military virtues to the wider civic order.

Military virtues and civic culture

The armed forces are increasingly an outpost of traditional virtues in a modern liberal society. Indeed, in many ways the services themselves have become organized according to liberal principles and market values. In sociological terms this transformation has generated a good deal of work on what has been called the shift from 'institution to occupation'.[17]

An institution is legitimised not in terms of its instrumental value to the needs of individual consumers/users but with reference to an overarching social purpose. As Charles Moskos has argued,

> Members of an institution are often seen as following a calling captured in words like duty, honour and country. They are commonly viewed and regard themselves as being different or apart from the broader society . . . Military service tradition-ally has acquired many institutional features, for example, fixed terms of enlist-ment, liability for 24 hour service, frequent moves of self and family, subjection to military discipline and law, and inability to resign, strike, or negotiate working conditions. When grievances are felt, members of an institution do not, as a rule, organize themselves into interest groups. Rather, if redress is sought it takes the form of personal recourse to superiors, with its implication that the organization *takes care of its own.* Above and beyond these conditions, of course there are the physical dangers inherent in combat training and actual combat operations. [emphasis added][18]

Normally, it is accepted that armed forces are ideal typical institutions. Traditional military values such as respect for authority, sense of duty, team-work, trust, cohesion, self-discipline and self-sacrifice, honour and concern for others are critical to operational effectiveness. Thus the functional requirements of combat lead to all armed forces having similar structural and cultural features. For example, a 'top-down' vertical hierarchy of ranks and order of command; and a distinctive institutional way of life with its for-mal colleges, internal laws and ethics, as well as informal rituals, all of which emphasise the importance of traditional values such as courage, manliness, dedication, and service and, above all, subordination of individual self-interest to the interest of the collectivity—i.e., the service and, ultimately, the state.

Institutions versus occupations

In contrast to institutions, occupations are organized and legitimised in terms of the logic of the market place. As Moskos argues, the military implications of an occupational model are profound. First, from the standpoint of assessing cost effectiveness, there are no major differences between military and civilian business organizations—the armed forces are not that special. Secondly, the most efficient way of organizing affairs is in terms of the cash nexus. Therefore all kinds of traditional 'in kind' payments and allowances or subsidies (for education, food, health, and welfare) are inappropriate. Thirdly, it is more efficient to reward people according directly to their technical skill and the state of the market and not to have these differentiations blurred by overall considerations of rank and seniority.[19]

Overall, the causes of occupationalism are fairly clear. First, the nuclear revolution and now, in this media age, the interest of public opinion in international affairs (or at least politicians' perceptions that it is) means that the military, more than ever before, have to share their work with other civilian groups, including diplomats and politicians. This establishes a context for civilian scrutiny of what the military does in general. Secondly, the continuing revolution in technology means that the military is increasingly dependent on a variety of civilian specialists for the effective development, running, and repair of its equipment. Thirdly, the pressure on defence budgets means that politicians have sought to squeeze more value out of costly defence budgets—a process that the end of the Cold War has exacerbated.[20] Fourthly, value change has had a dramatic impact on all traditional institutions, including the armed forces. Many of the influences once supportive of positive attitudes towards authority have waned, particularly with regard to the family, education, and religion. This means that the armed forces' core institutional values are no longer as firmly rooted in wider society, particularly concepts such as duty, self-discipline, self-sacrifice, respect, and concern for others. Legislation and public attitudes are now much more based on rights-based ethics than they were two decades ago. Whatever their basis—sexual, political, or religious preference, ethnicity, and so on—groups express rights of freedom and self-expression, and ask for any barriers to such expression to be removed. At the same time, not only are wider social obligations minimised or regarded as unac-

125

ceptable intrusions into areas of individual freedom, but any weaknesses in this area, e.g., criminal conduct, are not normally recognised as individual moral failings but attributed to some wider socio-economic factor. For these groups, 'Society' is merely an administrative vehicle for the realisation of these rights, not itself a sacred canopy of obligation: society is a means not an end.

The effect of occupationalism on military effectiveness

The indications of 'occupationalism' in many Western armed forces, including the British in recent years, are clear. Greater value for money is being sought from what is being spent through the introduction of cost centres and devolved budgets, civilianisation, market testing, and contracting-out of administrative and support functions. Military hierarchies are also being reviewed in order to see whether lessons of leaner and flatter structures from the business world can be applied to the military in order to achieve more cost-effective performance. Women are now excluded from very few occupations within the military, especially in the Navy and Air Force, where the combat roles are open to them. The exclusion of homosexuals from military service will have to be reviewed again despite the latest fudging exercise whereby homosexuality is regarded officially as incompatible with service but, normally, homosexuals will be administratively discharged so long as they are not committing acts that are illegal under the civilian legal code. Standards of discipline and tough training have to take into account wider civilian sensibilities (e.g., the future of boxing in the services is now in some doubt) and, in general, it is to be expected that any military tradition can only gain civilian society's acceptance if the military can successfully argue a case in court that operational effectiveness will be compromised if it is not retained.[21] Performance pay is openly mooted while traditional terms and conditions of service are currently under review, e.g., boarding school allowances. There is now open debate on the merits of a federation for military personnel in order for them to have a greater voice in, if not power to negotiate on, terms and conditions of service.[22] In this, those pressing for such an innovation make the not unreasonable judgement that without it the military will fare far worse than, say, the police did in connection with the Sheehy Report on their conditions of service.

In scholarly as well as policy debates about occupationalism in a military context, one of the critical questions has been: will this process have a negative impact on military effectiveness? It has been suggested that an excess of occupationalism will, for example, promote 9-5 attitudes to work, too much reliance on civil contract law in order to gain compliance with requests for logistic and related support from contractors in time of emergency; promote instrumental, self-interested orientations to work when the special nature of the military contract requires recognition and acceptance of the principle that operational success may require self-sacrifice and ordering others that this too is their duty.

Clearly some of these fears have been exaggerated or ill-founded, being based on prejudice, speculation, and far too little evidence. As David Segal has suggested, just because a soldier is concerned with pay and conditions of service or indeed looks to a military career as a stepping stone to social and economic advancement elsewhere in civilian life later on does not make that person necessarily an ineffective soldier.[23] Furthermore, some problems, for example, in making a success of gender integration in military and police organizations may well disappear with time when such integrated teams have grown used to the idea and chauvinistic attitudes by men towards women have been removed through training programmes. On the other hand, it is difficult to deny that a wholly occupational military is unlikely to be effective because of the special requirements of military life. Core traditional values are critical for operational effectiveness. The real issue is to identify these and show that they are necessary. In today's social climate, a successful defence of tradition rests on scientific and pragmatic defence.[24]

Cohesion, loyalty, and integrity in the military

All armed forces in liberal societies are having to establish where to draw the line between occupational and institutional values within their organizations. While the armed services cannot be separate from wider society, the key question is to identify those aspects of modern social life which must not be allowed to undermine unity, cohesion, and loyalty within the armed forces, that is to say the development of close bonds within military groups and between them and their leaders.

Such close bonds can only be forged if comrades have mutual trust and confidence in each other and with their superiors. The military necessity for all legal orders to be obeyed without question means that leaders giving such orders have to be trusted and must therefore have earned that trust by exhibiting the highest standards of integrity, and personal standards of behaviour. By integrity, one means being honest, reliable, caring of others, and being just in one's dealings with subordinates and peers. This is why drunkenness, drug abuse, indebtedness, all forms of dishonesty, bullying, racial and sexual discrimination or harassment are regarded as unacceptable within the British armed forces. The same can be said, for the moment at least, of homosexuality because it is perceived to undermine group cohesion and the relations of command and obedience because of the intrusion of real or perceived sexual favouritism or loyalties. Adultery within the military community is regarded as unacceptable for similar reasons: personnel on deployment who are concerned about their partners at home can hardly be expected to be fully operationally effective. With regard to adultery with members of the wider civilian community, this too is regarded as unacceptable because it indicates that military personnel are falling below the standard of integrity required of their role and thus bringing not only themselves but the institution of which they are a part into disrepute—an easy thing to do when public opinion is so eager to find fault or to prove the existence of hypocrisy. Accordingly, breaches of this and other moral standards in military communities result in ostracism, social exclusion and, ultimately, the dishonour and ignominy of dismissal from the service.

The military as an example of morality to society

Discussions of institution and occupation within a military context have largely assumed that the main questions to be addressed are, first, how far can traditional institutional features be removed in order to provide more cost effective performance in military organizations and secondly, what are the minimum institutional features required by the armed forces to be operationally effective and yet sufficiently attuned with wider liberal social values?

Yet a neglected line of argument is to ask another question: in what ways can the maintenance of key traditional military values not only provide the basis of effective armed forces but also contribute to the reconstruction of civic culture? This need not entail a commitment to a 'militarisation' of society which, I believe, would be both objectionable and impractical. Traditional military values, as outlined above, serve a wider social purpose because of the role of the armed forces in state and society as the ultimate 'public organization'. The modern state's territorial authority—its power to control territory and population from internal subversion and external threat—rests, ultimately, on the coercive power of its armed forces. In all states, the unique demands of preparing for and conducting military operations underpin the military's preoccupation with sustaining institutional values. In this sense all militaries are alike and identify with each other. In addition, armed forces are the ultimate guarantor of the values that underpin the society they are duty bound to defend, as expressed in its constitutional arrangements, core values, and conventions. This is what gives armed forces their distinctive 'national' characteristics. Occasionally, with revolutions, this requires a dramatic period of institution-building as is currently under way in Central and Eastern Europe, with old Communist ways being dispensed with and standards of liberal democratic civil-military relations being established. There is a third layer of values within the armed forces which is highlighted in modern democratic societies: the armed services are public service organizations with a unique contract—the duty to offer their lives for their country if required. In so doing they dramatise the standards to be expected in all areas of public life. As the ultimate guarantors of the state, it is the duty of all military personnel to support standards of conduct and respect for the law not only for their own operational effectiveness but also to maintain the respect of wider society. In return, through displaying key moral virtues, they provide society with exemplars of conduct to be expected of a civic society. That which is a special responsibility of public life should in any case enter into everyday social relations, care for others, honesty, integrity, and so forth. What the armed forces do, in part, is to remind members of modern society that key traditional military virtues still have a place in wider civilian society even if it is accepted that, necessarily, there must be a divergence between how the services operate and the ways of civilians.

The essential integrating force in the military and society—trust

One of the most important lessons for civilian society offered by military organizations is that society cannot be organized purely on the basis of exchange relations. Military society rests on moral foundations—even mercenary formations in history have possessed many of the military values that I have focused on, although not, of course, the ideal of exclusive service to one client—the state.

A key aspect of military society concerns relations of mutual trust and respect between comrades and leaders and led. It is an illustration of Durkheim's argument that *any* society cannot afford to dispense with altruism. Without trust, social relations become extremely brittle because each party to the relationship becomes preoccupied with devising arrangements to safeguard their interests should the other renege on their obligations or commitments; investigating whether the other's conduct is disreputable; devising bureaucratic mechanisms to ensure that the other performs as he should. Life becomes less efficient, less humorous, and more tedious and, to use an Americanism now, revealingly, being used more widely in the UK, litigious. And yet, with doubts about professional authority, to be litigious is merely to raise another question, can *this* lawyer be trusted?

It is no accident that, as a result of the attempt to organize social life as a market, all institutions, and the professional classes who work in them, have been invaded by a new wave of bureaucratic reporting mechanisms. Those who are not trusted to perform have to spend more time not performing but proving they have indeed performed well. Thus professionalism is increasingly viewed cynically as a hypocritical defence of vested producer interests. Professionals everywhere find that their traditional monopoly powers are being eroded as they face far higher levels of competition in providing services to clients than in the past. As we have seen in the discussion of institution and occupation, the distinctive culture of professional organizations is being undercut by the assumption that business is business in all contexts.

At the same time all professional organizations are experiencing an increase in client power. For example, in the military context there are far stricter mechanisms for the oversight and control of how resources are spent. Professionals have a choice: acquire financial skills or watch decisions critical to their work being taken by those who do have such skills. Efforts to obtain greater value for money account for many of these arrangements. Yet their introduction has only been possible because of a broader scepticism about the validity of claims of professional authority—a scepticism which in regard to public sector professionalism has hardly been discouraged by those who believe market exchange is the basis of a moral society. In the space created by this process of erosion, is a climate of distrust and more bureaucracy: thus as the traditional relations of trust between political elite and military personnel break down, it is hardly surprising to see, as noted earlier, attempts to organize a federation to defend service interests in the bureaucratic politics of resource allocation.

This erosion of professional authority is, I believe, connected with the broader context of new times I referred to earlier. The combination of a multipolar and a multicentric world has meant that *all* sources of authority are open to challenge from conflicting or alternative authorities.[25] Jacques clearly views this situation as liberating and indeed to be celebrated. But there is a cost: the need for confident leadership and professional judgement across all our institutions—the church, politics, the law, finance, and the military—in these difficult new times is increasing precisely at the same time that the capacity for such leadership to be rooted in reasonably stable moral authority is being undermined. One must not underestimate the seriousness of this challenge.

CHAPTER 11

The Fear
Of
Disrepute

William B. Allen

Modern men are afraid of pain: once they would endure it to avoid shame

Shaftesbury wrote that 'profound thinking is many times the cause of shallow thoughts'.[1] In thinking of the weakness of shame to control personal conduct in modern times, I find it hard to resist the thought that the shallowness of that modern philosophy, against which Shaftesbury wrote, contributed mightily to produce this incongruous result in souls shaped by nature to respond to the sting of shame as the ass responds to the sting of the whip by getting on with business.

What sober mind failed to note, as the case of Michael Fay unfolded in Singapore, the singularly obsessive and shallow fear a caning evinced in the Western world, especially in the United States? At moments it appeared that even capital punishment might be better tolerated than the deliberate infliction of bodily pain in repayment for social malefaction. Men were not always so tender, and it stands to reason that whatever accounts for their having become so may bear some relation to the utter loss of a generalised fear of social stigma (other than the fear of being found politically incorrect). Indeed, in proportion as the fear of pain inspires ever more powerful aversions in human beings, shame increasingly becomes a toothless tiger.

It was not always so. The case of Colonel Lewis Nicola displays an earlier standard. This brave soldier's 'sin' was to imagine George Washington as his country's rightful tyrant rather than its father. Washington's stern, angry rebuke to Nicola so stung the Colonel that Nicola never recovered. Successive abject apologies did not relieve his mind of the shame he felt for

133

having suggested that the army should make Washington monarch to relieve the country's distress.

The moral collapse of elites: does money reform?

Perhaps it will be thought inappropriate to raise examples of the well-bred, in order to open a discussion of contemporary social problems which generally take the ill-bred and lower classes as the subjects of inquiry. The familiar modern line of reasoning runs from an ill such as bastardy to poverty to crime to great poverty to great crime; the thought is that from the cause the effect surely follows, and the cause transcends or at least remains indifferent to character. The well-bred, accordingly, need never become *problems* and face only the danger of becoming victims.

I would maintain, however, that the well-bred in every era never have greater resources to bring to bear on critical social ills than they dispose of for their own affairs. The chief resource of the best bred in our own time seems to be money, and characteristically money is the medicine repetitively applied in efforts to cure social ills. Bastardy produced aid to unmarried mothers. Drug addiction summoned therapeutic rehabilitation. Chronic pauperism and unemployment spawned entitlements, training programmes, and public sinecures—whenever the rare impulse to demand responsibility from recipients of public charity could be heard. In the United States very recently, legislation euphemistically designed to 'get tough on crime' had to be paid for with so-called 'preventive programmes' whose premise is that public welfare could distract potential criminals from their waywardness. Today the prime asset social elites possess is money (even if not so inexhaustibly as utopians imagine) and they apply it liberally to salve social ills without ever reforming personal conduct.

I prefer, accordingly, to inquire where the well-bred went astray? In other words, what are the alternative foundations for the necessary work of reforming patterns of social conduct which materially undermine conditions of social stability?[2] On this occasion, specifically, I inquire why shame—the fear of disrepute—no longer serves to shape conduct and whether its power can be restored.

Welfare incentives to good behaviour may produce bad behaviour

Normally men employ attractions and aversions—incentives and disincentives—to motivate human beings toward desirable conduct. It may seem immaterial whether one employs incentives or disincentives, so long as the end be attained. Increasingly, however, certain dysfunctional behaviours seem intractable to every incentive and disincentive. It is easier to understand why incentives in general may fail. Where incentives alone prevail, relationships of *de facto* bribery or extortion evolve. That is, when 'a' attaches a buy-out price to 'b's' avoiding certain behaviours, it is in 'b's' interest progressively to worsen his behaviour, thereby increasing the pay-off required to control it. As an economist might put it, there is no equilibrium price that can be established, for any price attached to averting a little 'b' necessarily implies a higher price attached to averting a lot of 'b'. The social welfare principle always buys more of what it is willing to pay for, for 'b' has a well nigh infinite capacity to worsen his behaviour.

Would disincentives work better?

Perhaps disincentives would work better, reversing the pattern. The usual disincentives, however, depend entirely on men's conceptions of, first, the bases of human actions and, secondly, the ready availability of methodologies to apply them. Pain is a disincentive but is, in fact, less generally available than one might imagine. Stigma is a theoretical methodology but, in fact, is either not used or is not currently effective for particular reasons. In the remainder of this chapter I review the situation *vis-à-vis* these two methodologies and the potential for a revival of either or both. We must weigh the ineligibility of pain and the impotence of stigma.

Liberalism versus character

Stanley C. Brubaker argued in 1988 that 'the ability to punish criminals is part of a larger moral experience that is lost with liberalism's expulsion of the human good from politics'.[3] This seems to be what Selbourne means in arguing that contemporary citizenship is 'a catalog of "absolute rights" without corresponding "ethical duties" . . . a "corrupted liberal order" where citizens have turned into "ethical strangers" . . .'[4] Brubaker, however, maintains a principle of logical necessity, descending from the liberal order's attempt to remove anger from public life, and its correlative focus on the individual rather than the community.[5] Most importantly, however, comprehensive punishment 'inflicts pain on the criminal distinct from what is necessary for deterrence or rehabilitation'.

Liberalism (and Brubaker means Lockean liberalism) turns punishment into a proportionate tariff on unacceptable behaviours instead of a statement about an individual's character, because liberalism mediates all statements about character by means of conceptions of personal goals. It is only the *effect* of the personal goal—not the goal itself—which commands social reprehension. To swear at the inanimate object that bruises one's toe becomes equivalent to swearing at the criminal who steals one's cloak. Liberalism, then, does not prohibit ill-doing, it merely penalises it. Pain is not regarded as an apt penalty, and even the price of one's life must be rendered as painlessly as possible.

By drawing from Locke, Brubaker explains why pain is ineligible under liberal theory, but he does not adequately say why. He does not explain the connection between the ineligibility of pain *and* the impotence of shame. Beyond the formal constructs of philosophical systems, as Shaftesbury explained, it is necessary to touch the transforming psychological roots of these principles. He did not, however, explain why pain came to be regarded exclusively as material or physical pain.

The impotence of shame

Thomas Hobbes identified the powers of lust and repulsion or 'appetite and aversion' as the pillars of human conduct. In doing so he balanced fear and love or friendship as effective motivations among human beings. At the same time, however, Hobbes made it clear that appetite was narrower than love, focusing mainly on the sensation of pleasure, while aversion was focused mainly on the sensation of pain (and thus rightly called fear). Hobbesian materialism introduced to the modern era the possibility that human conduct could be regulated with resort to the powerful positive and negative forces of pleasure and pain.

Regarding pain, however, an interesting thing occurred. The fear which disposes men to avoid painful exigencies, now understood only in material and not in social terms, becomes a much narrower construct than would have operated in the sons of a Brutus in ancient Rome. When Brutus surrendered his sons to the laws of the state, stifling every paternal affection, he provided a powerful lesson to every other father and son. He did this because the pain of shame was a more powerful motivation than the pain of losing his sons to execution. In those earlier days, fear was a much bigger word, the kind of word that caused an Antigone to respond to an Ismene that execution at the hands of the state terrified her far less than the shame of infidelity to her family. Ismene was afraid, and called cowardly by her sister. But Antigone was no less afraid to dishonour her family.

The fear which motivates upright conduct has no share in the fear of pain, for often enough it fosters a willingness to endure pain in order to avoid shame. Since the age of materialism has spread so generally throughout the world, however, it is almost only the fear of pain which is felt by individuals. So social conduct is largely unrestrained precisely in those areas where fear alone could operate to restrain conduct. For example, schoolchildren in urban areas rarely fear their parents learning of their delinquencies (as once was true) so much as they fear falling victim to their fellow delinquents. So they arm themselves and shoot.

Juvenile crime: juveniles fear the pain their peers threaten them with more than the shame of their parents

Peer group pressure is often evoked to explain much youth behaviour. But peer group pressure would only be an impoverished version of the system of moral restraints in a mature society. Do the young truly respond from a fear of losing the respect of their peers, or do they respond in a world characterised by a vacuum of respect? Actually what looks like peer group pressure is nothing but the line of least resistance consistent with personal tastes for pleasures and pains. The only way to alter this pattern is to re-establish the vigorous operation of a fear of shame. Some modern Brutus must demonstrate for his weaker-willed fellows what it means to be dishonoured by one's sons, in order for a healthy, social fear to recover its power to guide human conduct.

All this is true because men may reason to just conclusions about human nature from the outward signs of human conduct. Hobbes and Locke turned men towards personal goals and feelings as autonomous and therefore arbitrary. As such, our reasonings about human conduct—in this light, better called behaviour—had to turn on principles more steady, namely, material interests. This move deprived men of every opportunity systematically to apply the levers of duty and shame as regulators of human conduct. Scientific inquiry itself eschewed all concern with gross behaviour in search of inner and even unconscious sources of motivation.

A science of proper conduct: fears and excuses

The last substantive occasion offered to men in the West to make gross behaviour the foundation of judgements about human conduct (and character) took shape in the novels of Jane Austen. The thrust of that lesson was imaged pithily in chapter five of *Emma*, when Mr. Knightley interrupted long and painful speculations on a case of foul weather that would prevent visiting families returning from dinner at the Randalls with the report that he had simply stepped out of doors to have a look, upon which he could confirm that there was not 'the smallest difficulty in their getting home'. His empirical manner had dissolved what to all others had seemed an unpleas-

137

ant moral dilemma. Gross empiricism overcame refined speculation and reconciled the parties to their duty. The novel itself, of course, has much to do with distinguishing evident signs of character from nuanced interpretations of motive.

Cultures in which shame retains its vitality operate much in the manner of Knightley's gross empiricism—a person is taken to be and treated for what he obviously does rather than what he purposes. Neither are freighted explanations of conduct founded in material or emotional inducements to ill conduct sufficient to offset palpable judgements of malefaction. So high a standard—no excuse is acceptable—is bound to induce fear of the consequences being thus exposed.

A forgotten moral language: taking shame seriously

Whether we today can recapture some of the regulative power of shame and stigma to address chronic social ills depends on the ability of the best among us to refit our vocabularies for the purpose. It will not do to affect an innocence long since lost. The scientific posture renders scepticism about the human good an indefinite companion to our moral reasonings. It must follow, then, that shame can reassume its power in human affairs only in so far as science and art can discover anew grounds to take it seriously.

Jane Austen's coaching failed of its mark when science discarded reason as a tool for weighing gross conduct. Modern science abandoned a science of moral characteristics for a science of general human behaviour. In this light, Marxism was not a radical break but only the perfection of a theory of exogenous explanation of human behaviour—not an extreme but the last step in a graduated process. Today the only positive methodology which seems open to the possibility of a science of moral characteristics is that variant of what is called public choice analysis which takes as its object of inquiry the actual conduct—as opposed to the ideologies, purposes, or visions—of public officers. It is more than an application of micro-economic principles to public decision-making. It is more deeply founded on the premise that collective action is explicable only by recourse to the particular interests of office-holders.

This interest remains that which is found in the impoverished version of liberalism. It possesses the distinctive characteristic, however, of being nakedly exposed without further authority to which to point as determining condition of the shape it takes. As such, it invites common sense appraisal as worthy or unworthy. Thus, this version of public choice creates a model which may, in turn, be applied to any human conduct. This is the positive theory that would fulfil Austen's implied positive science of moral propriety, and it becomes possible only when we recognise that a scepticism as to ends does not entail a scepticism as to moral capacities.

I do not pretend that this version of public choice is a mature moral science. As yet it has not progressed beyond applying rational choice principles to focus a moment of moral determination in the individual rather than in a reduction beneath the level of the individual. At present it has not advanced beyond trying to map all possible choices (game theory), while in principle the positive science of moral conduct should be able to identify stable characteristics and therefore patterns of explanation and judgement. Still, this model which refuses to try to guess what is going on inside the minds of individuals surpasses the prevailing methodology. The current exogenous model of analysis yields the paradigm introduced above: illegitimacy $\rightarrow$ poverty; poverty $\rightarrow$ crime; great poverty $\rightarrow$ great crime. In this model what is itself no evil, poverty, is locked in a cycle of explanation between the evils of bastardy and crime. What this model really says is that the evil of bastardy is poverty, and nothing else. The painful consequence is the only evil. When, therefore, illegitimacy couples with wealth, there is no evil. This is not a general explanation, whether of illegitimacy or of poverty; the putative connection based on a model of exogenous explanation is clearly wrong. Still, an inerrant human sense points to some explanation here that applies unfailingly. To find it we need to look at the individual, and at a science of proper conduct.

Where men today hesitate to judge one another's views of the human good, they freely indulge such judgements of similar views that take the form of governmental action. Accordingly, any systematic analysis of governmental action which can assimilate such action to the conduct of human beings in general will provide an instrument whereby to recover robust analysis of personal conduct. In that situation shame can recover its vitality, and where shame recovers vitality, the fear of shame can become a regulator of social conduct. By example, if we can succeed in producing a systematic analysis of the architects of welfare liberalism in terms not of their supposedly benevolent goals, but in terms of their actual conduct, then we could no less surely reprehend the conduct of the supposed beneficiaries of welfare liberalism. That is the starting point for a reappraisal of social conduct, in which we stand of such great need today.

CHAPTER 12

Learning to Love the Good in Community

Linda Woodhead

What are the springs of human action? Love and fear

On his right hand Billy tattooed the word 'love'
and on his left hand was the word 'fear'.
And in which hand he held fate
Was never clear

Bruce Springsteen

What is it that makes us moral? Since the moral life is not just one aspect of our lives, but the whole of those lives viewed from the perspective of right and wrong, good and bad, it is helpful to begin by asking about the basic dynamics of human life. All moral theories and all forms of moral discipline and formation rely on explicit or implicit understandings of what it is which drives human life, for only if the springs of human action are properly identified will it be possible to influence that action.

It is common for modern systems of morality to identify the will as the crucial force in human life, but close attention to the actual texture of human lives gives little support for this. In fact it seems that we exercise our wills relatively infrequently, and that even when we do so the will may often turn out to be a frustratingly impotent force against the much stronger currents which move us. I can will to give up alcohol or to stand up to my boss, but my desire for alcohol or my fear of losing my job often proves the much stronger force.

It seems, then, that the forces of love and fear are much stronger than the will and much more important in our lives. (Hate, a possible third force, though intermittently powerful, seems less prominent in normal circumstances.) Love directs all of us in greater or lesser measure, and many of us have one great love which controls us. Honest enquiry can reveal the object of this love—be it money, or status, or power, or spouse, or family, even a house and possessions. Likewise, most of us are also much affected by fear. For some people fear has a clear object—other people, public exposure, ridicule, failure, loss of what is loved. For others it is more inchoate, but powerfully influential none the less.

Both love and fear are relational, they relate us to something outside ourselves. But whereas fear is a centripetal force which turns us inward and *away* from the source of fear, love is a centrifugal force which turns us outward and *toward* what is loved. The centrifugal force of love was displayed by the Samaritan who went to the aid of the man fallen among thieves—he thought only of his neighbour. Those who passed by on the other side displayed the centripetal force of fear—they thought only of themselves. Whilst some of us may be driven *only* by love or *only* by fear, most of us seem to be driven by a mix of both. Like Billy in the Springsteen song, we may even become the battleground for mastery by one or the other.

Many moral disciplines work by harnessing fear: the fear of physical harm and shame

Since love and fear seem to be the chief engines of human action and inaction, they have a crucial importance in moral formation. Moral systems and forms of moral discipline will only work if they can harness one or other of these drives; they will work if they can make us afraid of what is wrong or, conversely, if they can make us love what is good.

Many attempts to make people moral—or at least law-abiding—try to harness fear. Most obviously, the civil law works in this way. Many citizens obey the laws of the state out of fear of the punishments which can be inflicted on them if they do not. The punishments can be social (the shame of being known to be a convicted criminal) and/or physical (loss of life, of wealth, of liberty).

A little more subtly, communities of all sorts and sizes make and keep their members moral by harnessing their fear of rejection or disapproval by other members of the group. Some communities may have institutional channels for expressing this disapproval (through a council of local elders, for example). Others, like local communities in the contemporary West, will be more likely to express social disapproval in less formal ways; but pointed gossip and the 'cold shoulder' can still have a very powerful effect. To lose one's 'respectability' in the local community may be an almost tangible experience, even today.

It has been suggested that loss of fear may be a cause of the moral collapse of contemporary society

A number of social, moral, and political commentators searching for reasons for the apparent moral collapse of contemporary society point to the loss of fear of wrong-doing in Western society as an important part of the explanation. Some see the dissipation of fear as the result of the growing ineffectiveness of the civil law and its agents. They argue that too few crimes are detected, and that even when they are, punishment is rarely adequate. In this they echo popular sentiment: the call for stronger policies on 'law and order' is increasingly heard at all levels of society, and politicians of all hues are falling over one another in trying to respond to it. In the face of a moral collapse which few are now willing to deny, the most common response is to call for measures which will make people more afraid of committing crimes.

Other commentators, including many of the contributors to this volume, point out that the state is not the only body which is able to engender a fear of wrong-doing, and argue that it is important to recognise and support other ways of accomplishing this end. In particular they emphasise the important role which smaller scale communities can play in making people moral through fear. It is rightly pointed out that a society without families, churches, or local communities will find it impossible to use social sanctions to discipline its members and will have to fall back on the state's cruder and more costly methods of engendering fear.

But is the use of fear to make people moral desirable?

The reintroduction of fear in society and the use of such fear to attach people to the virtues may seem at first sight to be the easiest and most effective way of responding to moral crisis. Yet the strategy is highly problematic.

There is little doubt that it is within the power of modern states to engender a fear which can prevent people from committing crimes and immoral actions; our knowledge of the Communist regimes of this century and of the effects of their collapse leave us in little doubt about this. But there is equally little doubt that the cost is huge. It is huge in economic terms—the vast number of people and institutions given over to the task of enforcing 'law and order' in the Communist bloc is just beginning to emerge. And it is huge in moral terms—the infringement of human liberties, the sacrifice of human lives, and the distortion of the truth are just part of the price to be paid.

So although the use of state power to stem lawlessness may initially seem attractive, the danger is that the state and its agents will end up a cause as well as a symptom of the moral collapse which brought them into being. Should we then rely instead on smaller scale communities to perform the same function? There seems little doubt that historically such communities have been effective in moral formation; societies without police forces had nevertheless very effective ways of policing themselves. Yet the question remains whether it was solely through fear that these communities achieved moral results. The chief reason for doubting this is that whilst fear seems quite effective in inhibiting vice, it seems much less effective in inculcating virtue. Whilst it is clear that social stability has always depended to some extent on the use of fear, it is much less clear that the same has been true for morality. Fear may be effective in containing sin, but is it really effective in eliminating it from the human soul? Having a society in which people do not steal because they are afraid of social disapproval or of the criminal justice system is better than having one in which people do steal, but it is not as good as having one in which people do not steal because they know it to be wrong. The absence of theft may indicate the existence of a stable society, but it does not necessarily indicate the existence of a virtuous one. Its stability is only as strong as its sanctions.

Christianity has been one of the most important influences on moral formation in the West and it stresses that love, not fear, should have the primary role

The suspicion that communities, unlike the state, make only limited use of fear in moral formation is borne out by considering the example of the most morally influential of them all in the West—the church.

At first sight it may seem strange to suggest that Christianity shuns the use of fear in attaching people to the virtues. Even a cursory reading of the Bible reveals its belief that those who reject God and do evil face terrible consequences—either in this world or the next. The Jesus of liberal imagination who calls everybody a child of God is very far from the Jesus of the Gospels who warns 'hypocrites' about 'the furnace of fire' and 'the outer darkness' into which they will be thrown and where there will be 'wailing and gnashing of teeth' (*Matthew* 12.42; 25.30).

Yet despite its belief that the wicked will be punished, it is striking how often the Bible refuses to use this belief as a threat to engender fear and so make people behave well. Rather, its characteristic approach is to emphasise God's goodness and grace in order to win an answering love and gratitude which will issue in good works. Thus the giving of the Ten Commandments begins with a reminder of why Israel should obey them—because 'I am the Lord your God, who brought you out of the house of bondage' (*Exodus* 20.2; *Deuteronomy* 5.6); love not fear should call forth obedience. Similarly, Jesus begins His ministry with a proclamation of the 'good news' of a gracious kingdom—in contrast to John the Baptist's bad news of 'the wrath to come' (*Matthew* 3.7). It is the good news of what God is doing and what He is offering which must win people for His cause, not the threat of His judgement. The Biblical message is not, behave well and you'll be blessed, but you've been blessed so behave well—you've been given a talent so use it well; you've been forgiven so forgive others; you've been loved so love.

That Jesus believed love to be the all-important force in the good life is borne out in the so-called double commandment, the most influential of Christian moral teachings. In response to the question, 'which is the greatest commandment in the law?' Jesus' reply is 'You shall *love*' . . . 'You shall love the Lord your God with all your heart, and with all your soul, and with all your mind . . . You shall love your neighbour as yourself. On these commandments depend all the law and the prophets' (*Matthew* 22.35-40 and parallels). Jesus teaches much more about love, but more importantly He embodies these teachings in the living of His life and the manner of His death, and it is to this enactment that Christians have always looked to find the true meaning of the commandment to love.

Far from emphasising the moral significance of fear then, Christian morality insists that actions motivated solely by fear are worthless. The message of the Bible is that love for God should exclude fear. As the First Letter of John says, 'There is no fear in love, but perfect love casts out fear' (4.18). The fear of God should remain, but this fear, far from being the opposite of love for God, is part of it. It is part of the proper response to God's infinity, His omnipotence, His majesty, His greatness, His goodness. It is not a timorous fear and does not exclude trust or joy—so the women run from the empty tomb with 'fear and great joy' (*Matthew* 28.8) and *Psalms* 115 exhorts, 'You who fear the Lord, trust in the Lord'. Far from being the centripetal force whose object is evil, fear of God is part of the centrifugal force whose object is good. Love, not fear, should make the Christian moral.

The goods which should be loved according to Christian tradition

Christianity regards the commandment to love not as arbitrary divine fiat, but as a directive about how to respond appropriately to reality. Since God and the world He has created are both good, love is the proper response to them. Love, then, is not a mere movement of will or emotion, but has an important cognitive element; it involves knowledge of what is good and the quest for such knowledge. And as a form of knowledge, it is possible for love to be mistaken.

Jesus warns about the dangers of false loves throughout His teaching. The love of money, the love of esteem, even the love of one's family may distract one from the true good. Not that all these objects of love are necessarily bad in themselves, but they must only be given their due. This belief that there is a hierarchy of goods and that love must be proportionate to their goodness became pervasive in Christian thought. To quote Augustine, 'What God has made for you is good; but some goods are great, others small: there are goods terrestrial, goods spiritual, goods temporal . . . Therefore it is said in scripture: "order in me love"'.[1]

The attempt to classify the chief goods of human life and the order of their goodness is one which is made in many works of Christian ethics and theology. Generally only God, neighbour, and (sometimes) self are classified as worthy of the love of one's whole heart. But it is recognised that there are many other goods worthy of love. Some of these are intrinsic goods, like the created world of plants and animals. Others are 'derivative goods', goods which are good because they serve higher goods—knowledge of God and human flourishing in particular. Certain human institutions are counted as derivative goods—the church, the nation, the family, property, and the law, for example.

Christian methods of inculcating love of the good

According to Christianity, knowledge of what is truly good is an essential first step in the moral life. Communication of such knowledge is therefore an important part of Christian moral formation. But since it is possible to know what is good but not to be changed by such knowledge, something more is required. Augustine calls this 'delight', explaining, 'It does not follow that we shall strive for that which we have recognised as worth our striving, unless we delight in it in the measure in which it is proper to be loved'.[2] So besides instruction about the good, Christian moral formation involves the cultivation of delight in and desire for the good.

Moral formation necessarily social

For Christianity, knowledge and love of the good can only be inculcated within a society of believers. Moral formation is never primarily an individual project, but a social one.

An important reason why this is so is that Christian moral formation depends upon tradition. The church's tradition is the accumulated wisdom (and perhaps unwisdom) of past and present Christian generations. Some of it will be written, but much of it will be passed down by personal contact— teachings, customs, manners, unquestioned and perhaps unconscious responses and habits of life all move from generation to generation in this way. Some of the tradition will be common to all churches, some of it specific to particular ones, to particular locales, and even to particular families. The possession of a tradition means that each individual does not have to start from scratch in attaining moral wisdom. Tradition is like a language: we need it in order to forget it and get on with our lives. As George Guiver puts it, 'a living future is only possible if it is the making new of a living inheritance'.[3]

An additional reason for Christianity's insistence on the social character of moral formation is its recognition of the importance of reinforcement, support, and help in moral development. As loving and mutually dependent beings, all humans feel a desire for their beliefs to be shared by at least some others and this seems especially true in the case of moral beliefs. Indeed, as the sociology of knowledge has convincingly shown, without such wider acceptance beliefs simply cease to be plausible. The support of other people is also crucial when hard decisions have to be made and conflict faced, and the help of others can bring new energy, insight, confidence, and hope.

Finally, Christianity's insistence that morality needs communities is bound up with its conception of the good for human beings. That good, as we have seen, consists in love, and love unites. The perfect human society, united by belief in God, is the goal which Christianity holds before humanity. It would be strange indeed if its moral formation did not begin as well as end with community.

Catechesis—learning what is good

Christianity employs various methods for imparting knowledge of the good. Straightforward teaching about faith and morals (catechesis) has traditionally been offered by the church as an essential step in becoming a

Christian, usually preceding baptism or confirmation. By the Middle Ages, books of catechetical instruction began to appear, often containing easily remembered moral instruction—lists of the seven deadly sins, the seven gifts of the Holy Spirit, the seven principal virtues, for example. The Reformation led to a renewed emphasis on the importance of catechesis in both Protestant and Catholic churches, and this combined with the invention of printing led to the introduction of new methods of Christian instruction—within the family, in the Sunday school, in lengthy and didactic sermonising, for example.

Besides catechesis, the most important source of a Christian's knowledge of good and evil is undoubtedly the Bible. Contrary to popular perception, the Bible's significance for moral instruction does not lie in its being a law code. The Bible does contain some clear commandments and prohibitions, but these make up only a tiny fraction of its content. In fact the Bible is an account of the world from its origins to its end, from God's point of view. It is by means of this account that the Bible gives moral instruction, for it shows its readers where reality and goodness lie and in what they consist. In particular, the Bible shows its readers 'the glory of God in the face of Christ' (2 *Corinthians* 4.6) and calls them to love what they have seen.

Worship—delighting in the good

It is through worship that Christians come not just to know what is good, but to delight in it and become conformed to it. This is a lifelong process and at its heart is participation in the church's liturgy—day on day, week on week, year on year.

Christian worship is about paying attention to the good. This attention takes two main forms: adoration and contrition. In adoration, Christians direct their gaze to God in love and gratitude. In contrition, they direct that gaze to themselves, but in the light of God, the true good. In this light 'no man can stand', and the worshipper confesses the ways in which he or she falls short of the good and asks for help in conforming to it more closely.

For most Christians the eucharist is the occasion at which the adoration and contrition of true worship become most possible and most real. The eucharist marks the first day of the week, and is the point at which a small portion of time, six days, can be reflected upon in the light of the good, celebrated and repented, and the coming week prepared for; the sabbath is the point at which the eternal intersects with the everyday and sacralizes it. In the eucharist the good is set before the people in readings, sermons, and prayers. In a general confession the people confess their failure to live up to the good, and receive absolution—the vital permission to start again without being tied down by previous wrong-doings.

The climax of the eucharistic service comes in the offering and taking of communion. The whole of what has preceded is summed up here, the good being not merely invoked, but (according to orthodox Christian belief) made present in the sacraments and given to those who receive them. God Himself comes down to earth in the sacraments, and with this gift He redeems His people, uniting them with Himself and one another in the communion which is their true good. Here good is not merely represented, but is made real in a community of goods, and it is every Christian's duty to maintain it in the everyday life to which he or she will shortly return.

In addition to shaping time around the weekly communion of goods, Christianity shapes it around a twelve-monthly cycle which is given form by its remembrance of the life, death and resurrection of Christ. As with the eucharist, so with the liturgical year, portions (like Lent) are given over to contrition, and portions (like Christmas and Easter) are given over to celebration and adoration. Other days are marked out by the remembrance of good lives, the lives of the saints. By living in this sacred time Christians conform their lives annually to the life of Christ and live their lives through His.

Whenever Christianity has tried to harness people's fear in the attempt to make them moral, the results have been shameful

It cannot be denied that in many of its historical manifestations Christianity has succumbed to the temptation to issue threats and harness fear in the attempt to attach people to virtue. The first notorious example of a prominent Christian to take this course is Augustine, and that he should have done so is remarkable, given his repeated emphasis that love, not fear, must rule in the Christian life. Yet when faced with a schism in the churches of North Africa where he was bishop, Augustine invoked a phrase from one of Jesus' parables—'compel them to come in' (*Luke* 14.23) to justify the use of force against the schismatics.[4] In doing so he became the father of all subsequent Christian leaders who have made use of threats ranging from excommunication to trial, torture, and death, to enforce right belief and right behaviour. Even where such methods were effective in achieving their ends, the immorality and destructiveness involved cast a shadow over the history of Christianity.

The development of a belief in hell, a place of eternal punishment, can also be seen as a means by which Christianity tried to attach people to the virtues by making them frightened. Though the development of belief in hell seems to be coincident with the development of Christianity itself, it was not always used as a threat to make people moral. Often it was used to speak of God's righteousness rather than His vengeance, and to reassure the powerless that their oppressors (including clergy) would get their just deserts. The use of hell as an instrument with which to terrify people into obedience seems to have become most common in the early modern period, a process which the historian Delumeau refers to as 'the hyper-culpabilisation of the West'. There seems little doubt that a growing obsession with sin, guilt, and hell in the 17th and 18th centuries had very destructive consequences not just for individual Christian men and women, but for the church as a whole.[5] Christianity has only been Christian when it has remained true to its insight that love, not fear, makes people moral.

Conclusion—we need to learn to love the good once more

Whether we are Christians or not, the Christian tradition is a useful reminder that love can and should have a much more important place than fear in moral formation. Clearly fear and the instruments of fear will always be necessary to restrain evil, to stop men 'devouring one another' as Luther put it,[6] but their ability to effect a real change and make people more moral is highly questionable. Only those who love the good, not those who fear punishment, will remain moral when their self-interest is threatened, when they know they could 'get away' with immorality, when social forces put pressure on them to behave badly.

Yet our society displays an increasing reluctance to love the good, even to admit that good exists. One of our worst faults is cynicism, and cynicism is nothing more than the refusal to believe that anything is good. We have become suspicious of everything. A 'hermeneutic of suspicion' has become an obligatory tool of the academic busily engaged in the task of 'deconstruction'. The 'investigative journalist' is only interested in hunting out and exposing corruption. The newspapers are quick to rubbish, to expose, to find fault, to reveal feet of clay. Our consumer culture celebrates the camp, the ironic, the sardonic. And now political correctness adds force to the reluctance to call anything in Western culture good for fear of 'oppressing' those who are not a part of it. Even health, learning, and happy family life can no longer be affirmed as goods for fear of offending those who do not enjoy them.

The only way to restore the moral health of our society is by overcoming this cynicism and unthinking relativism and learning once more to love as 'goods' those things we now affect to despise: God, neighbour, the natural world, church, nation, marriage, the family, institutions of learning, the law, property, local and national cultures, customs, mores, and so on. When soldiers in the two world wars said they were prepared to die for their country, it was usually these goods they had in mind. Their love of them was strong enough to overcome fear and to stand the ultimate test of death. It had been inculcated by the age-old techniques of Christianity of which I have tried to give some account above, and by a culture which still respected these goods and which, through education, through the law, through example, through broadcasting, through literature, made this respect plain.

Whether anybody would be prepared to die for the good today is a moot point. Yet this is not simply the fault of individual men and women. As Christianity recognises, individuals cannot learn to love the good on their own. To become and to remain moral it is necessary to have the support, guidance, and reinforcement of others. This means that it is necessary to belong to communities of goods in which we are taught what is good, united by our love of that good, and in that unity to embody the good. Introducing more fear in our society might be an effective way of managing the crisis in which we now find ourselves, but ultimately it can lead only to further social fragmentation. Learning to love the good once more is the only real hope we have for overcoming moral crisis and restoring our lost unity.

CHAPTER 13

Is Civic Order Possible in the Modern City?

Ross Lence

The crisis of public order in the modern city

To those inclined to the new way of thinking about cities and the science of urban politics, it may seem strange, if not presumptuous for a man whose favourite book is Thucydides' *The History of the Peloponnesian War* to undertake a study on the prospects for civic virtue in an urban environment. If an apology be necessary, suffice it to say that the problems of urban life are hardly new. Since the first founding of the city by Enoch—not coincidentally the son of Cain—there has been reason to suspect the moral capacities of urban man. And while some men, like the immortal Pericles, extol the virtues of the city, others argue that human nature as revealed in the plague of Thucydides seems a more appropriate image of urban living than some state of peace, progress, and stability.

In modern times no plague is necessary to reveal the Hobbesian character of man. The daily reports of death and mayhem are constant reminders of the imperfections of men. Each crime seems to be more heinous than the last: gang rapes and murders; random drive-by shootings; children killing parents; parents killing children; children killing children. Cannibals all, it would seem.

At every turn these monstrous acts have produced anguish and dismay. And at every turn politicians, in an effort to quell growing public unrest throughout Western democracies, have promised stiff new penalties and a restoration of law and order. Everywhere public concern seems to be on the rise. And everywhere the response is the same: more laws, more government, more police, more taxes.

157

Still, I ask you: who does not find it paradoxical that in Washington, D.C., the city of national government, and New York City, where two of the most stringent gun-control laws in America are in force, no one is safe to walk the streets by day or night without threat to body and soul? Who, except perhaps some dim-witted bureaucrat, believes the 'War on Drugs' has been won? And who believes that additional laws, increased police protection, and individual or community indignation can restore peace and order to Leeds, England, where a 14 year-old boy has terrorized the whole city by his rampage of villainy? Can there be any greater proofs of the failure of public policy than these?

Draconian solutions

Indeed, all evidence suggests that more draconian solutions may be necessary to restore public and private virtue than public policy makers have been willing to admit—solutions which will require bold new thinking, as well as considerable pain and dislocation. Among those things genuine searchers for social order may have to give up are the comforts and freedoms of the city, indeed maybe the very city itself. And make no mistake about it: one ought not to expect consensus on these solutions. To the contrary, like Machiavelli's Cesare Borgia before us, we may well have to employ the skilful services of a Messer Remirro de Orco—that cruel and expeditious man—who reduced Romagna to peace and unity.

Today the solutions advanced to solve the crisis of the modern city are as varied as are their proponents. Some claim that society is too permissive; others argue that society is too repressive. Some claim that the decline in society can only be reversed by a restoration of the old moral and religious codes; others claim that religion cannot be depended upon in modern times, and that the only real hope is to be found in the largely untested hypotheses of modern social science. Everywhere civil libertarians are vigilant guardians of the public trust, waiting to sound the alarm if any proposal is in conflict with their notion of the fundamental code or of the rights of the human person. Confusion and disorder are seen as much in our thinking as in our public streets. Societies everywhere find themselves at irreconcilable odds over what is to be done.

Listening to this debate one is led to appreciate the wisdom of Alexander Hamilton in *The Federalist* when he noted:

> Ambition, avarice, personal animosity, party, opposition, and many other motives, not more laudable than these, are apt to operate as well upon those who support as well as upon those who oppose the right side of a question.

158

And yet however just these sentiments will be allowed to be, we have already sufficient indications, that it will happen in this as in all former cases of great national discussion. To judge from the conduct of the opposite parties, we shall be led to conclude, that they will mutually hope to evince the justness of their opinions, and to increase the number of their converts, by the loudness of their declamations and by the bitterness of their invectives.[1]

In spite of the ensuing confusion of all the proposals and counter-proposals, the public knows one thing for certain: something is radically wrong with a public policy where people are not safe to walk the streets, where a policeman is reprimanded for boxing the ears of an impudent youngster, and where schools install metal detectors which cannot be activated until advance warning has been given as to the day and the hour they will be used. Indeed, the public has come to recognise contemporary public policy as little more than rearranging chairs on the deck of the *Titanic*— where anything and everything is allowed between and among consenting adults, except the shooting of firecrackers.

Is man willing to make sacrifices for social order or is the longing for it mere nostalgia?

Not so long ago, every American schoolboy knew, of course, of the axiom of Thomas Jefferson and the other Southern agrarians that there exists an inextricable tie between agrarian societies and virtue. Once the natural simplicity of rural life yielded the floor to urban life, public and private virtue were always endangered. Today, however, the story is relegated to the level of myth—either no longer possible, or no longer allowed.

Whatever the dangers of urban life, we do know that in modern times men have been fleeing rural communities in ever-increasing numbers, presumably not in pursuit of vice, but freedom. Indeed, if we judge men by their feet, rather than by their words, most men would prefer the freedom of the city to the security and civic virtue of the rural community, where Aunt Myrtle was posted as a sentry at the window to determine when we came in and where we had been. The city brings a new-found freedom of movement and commotion, where the gossip of neighbours and expectations of family are lost in the complexity of urban life. Men seem willing to risk life and limb rather than suffer the penetrating silence and imposed discipline of rural life.

It is in that context, then, that we say that the nostalgia for the old order may be just that: nostalgia. Men would, of course, prefer both the freedom of the city and the security of the rural community, but if one of the two must be lacking, it must be security. Their preference for the freedom and anonymity of urban life is unmistakable: men have never had more free-dom. Thus, while urban man cries out for a return to the old order—where a man did not lock his doors by day and slept with an open window by night (just like in the country!)—he is unwilling to allow the necessary restraints on his personal liberty to make such a condition possible.

The city source of so much 'civilization' and such uncivilized behaviour

Given this modern preference for the freedom and motion of urban living over the security and civic virtue of rural communities, must we necessarily conclude that the moral decay of our regime is irreversible and that civic virtue in an urban setting is not possible? Is the current cry for law and order not proof that the public will not long tolerate disorder? Is Attila really at the gates?

One cannot deny that the city has been condemned throughout history for its decadence, decay, violence, and villainy. Furthermore, there is considerable evidence to support the claim that societies have long had cycles of violence from which many have successfully recovered. Compounding all of this, of course, is the fact that charges of corruption and moral decay have been part of the vocabulary of the Anglo-Saxon tradition from the very beginning of the democratic era. Who has not heard the alarm of John Trenchard and Thomas Gordon, Fischer Ames, or Aleksandr Solzhentisyn?

Everywhere, the city of the West is condemned as crime-ridden and corrupt, yet that same city is the glory of Western civilization. Whoever thinks farmers are the force behind modern Western culture? Why, even the U.S. Census Bureau does not bother to count them any more. Cities are the glory of the West. The opera, the symphony orchestra, the theatre, the sporting arena, all of these are the consequence of urban life. It would not seem inappropriate to remind ourselves of the claims of the immortal Pericles, that for better or worse we have left behind us imperishable monuments to our greatness.[2]

Suppose that the modern city did indeed stand as the main obstacle to a return to social order. Suppose *it* had to be given up as the price of security. What a price that would be. Faced with that price, we might try to play down the disorder of the city. In matters such as crime, freedom, or public and private virtue, public opinion is often driven by perceptions, which can be deceived as well as deceiving. In the case of crime, for instance, violence in society may in fact be declining while public awareness of it is increasing. Public perception of an increase in crime may be no more than a more accurate or a more graphic reporting of violence in society. That theft, robbery, prostitution, and the like are everywhere antecedent to records is a truth for which no man needs evidence, but that these same irregular passions of men are everywhere in ascendance is not so obvious as some would have us believe.

Public perception of crime is also affected by the very definition of crime itself. As societies become increasingly complex and interdependent, there arises a need for the greater and greater extension of law. Matters which today must be defined as crimes of vandalism or the destruction of private property were little more than irritating pranks of youth in days gone by. What farmer living in Gibson county in southern Indiana did not dread the coming of Halloween and the yearly ritual of the over-turning of his out-house? It seems safe to assume on the basis of these observations (as well as numerous other concerns not mentioned), that perception is critical, if not determinative in our discussion of public order in an urban environment.

Exceptions and mitigations there are. Having acknowledged them, however, it is also good to remind ourselves that not everything is a matter of perception alone. Crime is still crime; violence against others is still violence; and, dare we say it, sin is still sin. While we must be cautious of our perceptions, we should not abandon our common sense. Myth and reality are not one and the same. Those who are easily confused about the difference will no doubt see the horror in that wonderful comic strip, 'The Wizard of Id', where the king announces from his balcony that he will reduce crime in the streets by 50 per cent. A doubting Thomas in the crowd remarks sceptically, 'How will he do that?' 'Simple', retorts one of the king's advisors, 'double the number of streets'.

Modern man wants both the freedom of the modern city and the order of the rural community

Given the tension between the call for draconian measures to restore public order on the one hand, and man's preference for the freedom of urban life to the confines of rural living on the other, it seems evident that what is needed is a bold new paradigm of civic virtue in an urban environment. Obviously in the confines of a few pages, it is impossible to construct a comprehensive theory. Nor is it possible to offer even an outline of the critical literature of urban politics, psychology, sociology, history, philosophy, and anthropology which is most relevant to our current understanding of the city.[3] It must suffice here merely to offer some preliminary observations on those matters which a thoughtful man would have to reconsider before con-

161

structing a new theory of public order and civic virtue in an urban setting. I will be content if those who follow behind my back find this pre-theory analysis useful in their own thoughts on these complex matters.

Does civic virtue require private virtue?

Of the many presumptions and convictions upon which the contemporary discussion of public order is founded, there are two which seem most in need of attention. The first of these presumptions is that the restoration of civic virtue will lead to the return of decency and public order. The second is that the source of the moral decline of modern times and the pervasive violence of urban life can best be explained simply in terms of some abnormality in the minds of men.

At one extreme is the civic virtue debate and those who think that social order can be restored by new and better institutional arrangements: better welfare, better policing, better government. For these people, politics and government can compensate for the moral deficiencies of men. Such thinking is, not surprisingly, popular amongst politicians, bureaucrats, and social scientists. Then there are those who admit that virtue may play some role but define it only by its results. Virtue is that behaviour, those habits, which maximise the chances of men 'living together in Peace, and Unity'.[4] Virtue is divided into public—that with public consequences—and private. Further along the spectrum are those who think that order depends on goodness. Increasing numbers of people have returned to the old way of thinking, that good men make good government; not good government good men. And men are not made good by self-proclamation, but by the exercise of virtue itself. Moral decline in civic virtue, then, can only be corrected by the restoration of virtue in the individual soul of man.

They are beginning to see that no real discussion of civic virtue can exclude the question of private virtue. Plato was one of the first men in the West to promulgate the notion that the souls of men and the character of the city are inextricably tied. As an oligarchy consists of oligarchic men, so democracy consists of democratic men—men who have democratic souls. It was in that context that his student, the philosopher Aristotle, asked the question whether it is possible for the good man to be a good citizen.

Even these people, however, do not really go to the end of the argument. They want order, and they want virtue, but they still hold back from acknowledging, let alone paying, its price. That price includes material goods, the wealth, purveyors, houses, restaurants of the modern city; culture, the architecture, the opera, the sophistication of the modern city; but most of all the freedom of the city: the cover of anonymity, the luxury of a private space in which individual desires are unchecked, the scope for autonomy.

Any restoration of public and private virtue will require considerable pain and readjustment in our actions, our commitments, and our beliefs. We must begin by re-examining the belief so very much in vogue these days, that the public should concern itself only with public behaviour and that whatever anyone declares to be self-regarding is a private matter. All claims of individual rights and personal liberties and freedom must necessarily be understood in the context of the greater public good, which of its very nature includes public order itself.

Urban ecology and the components of community life

One does not have to be an avid reader of William Faulkner to know, of course, that 'rural' living does not guarantee a sense of community. Thus, when we say that the crisis of the modern city is the crisis of community, we are not referring to some decline in 'meaningful inter-personal relationships' in an urban setting. At the same time, the sociological and psychological literature of modern social science would seem to be replete with evidence that small groups can be most efficacious in compensating the correlative needs of men.

If the crisis of the modern city is not necessarily a consequence of some deficiency in the psyche unique to urban men, then perhaps the problem with which we are dealing is one of a crisis of ecology: a tension between man and his environment. Social disorder does not spring from lack of virtue alone. Order requires not only the disposition of individuals to the practice of virtues, but an environment in which they can be practised. Some environments are more conducive to the practice of virtue than others. So even to concede the role of thoroughgoing virtue—rather than utilitarian virtue—does not go far enough. Being prepared to be good is not enough. One must be prepared to live in the place, the environment, in which goodness can indeed engender order. What, then, are the non-cognitive components of the environment that we can recognize as both the cause and effect of 'community'?

Or, to put the matter another way: what are the primary components of community life that made small towns of the recent past 'communities', independent of the particular persons of whom they were composed? Let me identify those which I believe are most critical.

163

- *Familiarity*: Probably the single most noted characteristic of small towns is familiarity with persons, location, and events. There seems reason to believe that there is an optimal number beyond which the number of persons cannot be increased without undermining this fundamental component of community life.
- *Continuity*: This familiarity is further reinforced by the fact that people in these small towns not only expect to interact with the same persons time and time again, but often do so in the same set of circumstances. These men in time become 'friends'.
- *Civic responsibility*: Because of the smaller number of persons involved in the decision-making and direction of the community, each individual is required to participate in more activities and events, and each person comes to realise that the success of the enterprise is dependent upon his fulfilling his assigned roles in the community. Hence, the small town is marked by a sense of civic responsibility and duty. A sizable body of psychological literature confirms what a thoughtful man knew, namely that as the number of persons increases, the individual energy and commitment decreases.
- *Comprehensibility*: Implicit in this sense of civic responsibility and duty is the matter of comprehensibility. Members of the community are far more likely to have a sense of the common goals and commitments, and to understand their role or functions in achieving those goals.
- *Manageability*: But comprehension alone is not sufficient. There must also be a sense of manageability. It is this component which allows the community to take the appropriate action to reward or to correct the behaviour of individuals within the community itself.
- *Predictability*: Because people have a sense of comprehensibility and manageability, they also develop a clear sense of expectation. They know what should happen, and how men will react.
- *Trust*: A more particular form of predictability, of course, is the matter of trust. Predictability allows the community to set standards of conduct for the measure of a man's integrity. Only those who fulfil their agreements or who have a shared sense of goals with the community are considered to be men of integrity and trust.
- *Pace*: Small towns are also well known for their pace of life. From the speed of the traffic, to the attention given to problems and events, small towns are marked by a moderate pace.
- *Simplicity*: The problems and issues that make up small-town living are

in general relatively simple. Distances are smaller, issues are less complex, and solutions are direct and easily understood.

- *Directness*: And finally, corresponding with this simplicity is a directness in dealing with matters at hand. Citizens are more apt to take corrective measures before intermediaries are needed to resolve disputes.

Modern cities do not provide the environmental conditions for virtue and order

Cities, at least modern cities, cannot provide these conditions. They are then, it would seem, incapable of community, not because of some abnormality in the minds of urbanites, but because of the ecological patterns of interaction necessitated by the sheer size of the city itself. Although many use the terms city, urban life, urban community, and urbanism interchangeably, this thesaurus-like approach to language is not without serious difficulties.

Aristotle was the first to warn us of the confusion which was certain to follow if one mistakenly identified Babylon as a *polis*. A walled enclosure which takes three days to cross cannot be a city properly understood. Men living together for the purposes of economic and political intercourse do not constitute a city because friendship under such conditions is not possible. Law becomes a mere guarantor of one man's rights against another's, and the focus of politics becomes mere life, instead of what it ought to be—the good life.

It is not my purpose here to defend the Aristotelian position on these matters. As troublesome as the modern understanding of public virtue may be, there are even more compelling reasons to believe that many of the conditions so critical to the ancient political orders are no longer possible in modern times, not the least of which is the number of people who must today be accommodated within political units.[5] Suffice it to say that while some still differentiate a city from a village on the basis of the presence or absence of a cathedral, the more common definition is in terms of some arbitrary number of persons living together within certain legally defined boundaries.

That is not to say, of course, that one cannot differentiate one city from another. It is still possible to speak of the 'images' of various cities,[6] and even the village idiot is expected to recognise the difference between London and, say, Topeka, Kansas. Still, if one were to control for obvious topographical differences on the one hand, and social, cultural, and political differences on the other, these cities may not be as differentiable as some would have us believe. Problems of crime, transportation, water resource

165

allocation, etc., are common to all cities. So uniform are these problems in fact, it is said that a man who only took the local shopping mall as his compass and guide would not be able to know if he were in Houston, Texas, or Whitefish, Montana.

Be that as it may, there can be no doubt that as cities get larger and larger, the differences between them become smaller and smaller. If we now compare the megapolis of modern times with the city of Aristotle, we are forced to conclude that the 'urbanism' of the megapolis of modern times has rendered inoperative the old meaning of the city. No longer is the city a community of free men, living together in friendship and pursuing the common good through shared values, shared commitments, and shared goals. The modern city has only one goal: functionalism. This functionalism is reflected in its art, its architecture, and its politics.[7]

The eclipse of civic virtue

Those who have taken pains to follow this study have, I hope, a clearer sense of the complex cluster of ideas raised by the question of public virtue within the context of an urban environment. The crisis of public virtue is in large measure a matter of perception founded upon, or driven by, a functional definition of virtue which is largely inconsistent with the traditional assumptions about the isomeric nature of public and private virtue on the one hand, and with the psychological components of urban ecology on the other.

And now we see the enormous distance between our own presumptions and those of contemporary public policy makers. No longer can we merely assume that a proper adjustment of public policy will produce a general consensus on the public or common good or that the source of today's crisis of public virtue is a simple manifestation of some abnormality in the minds of men.

In the case of civic virtue, our brief discussion suggests that the rise of the modern-day megapolis has necessitated a decline in friendship, which in turn has undermined the very foundation of the common good. Justice, the necessary substitute for this common good, has indeed become, as was adumbrated in the texts of Aristotle, little more than the protection of the political and civil rights of one individual against another. It is in this context that I have elsewhere so often likened contemporary politics to the radical redistribution of previously stolen goods.

In the case of our discussion of urban ecology, there is reason to believe that there are many cognitive and non-cognitive factors which radically influence the psyche of man, and that the individual may not be as responsible for his actions as was first thought. It is in the context of this complex, interactive web that we need to give serious thought to the possibility that the urban life of the megapolis is incompatible with public order and civic virtue: the modern city has nothing to replace the role of gossip, public reputation, and the *posse comitatus*. In that sense it may truly be said that we fiddle, while Rome burns.

Notes
&
References

Chapter 1

1. See, for example, Philip Rieff, 'The Newer Noises of War in the Second Culture Camp', *Yale Journal of Law and the Humanities*, 1991, Vol. 3, pp. 315–388; Robert Nisbet, *Twilight of Authority*, New York: Oxford, 1975.

2. See Quentin Anderson, *The Imperial Self*, New York: Knopf, 1971; and Anderson's 'Whitman's New Man', Introduction to *Walt Whitman's Revision of the Analysis of 'Leaves of Grass'*, New York: New York University Press, 1974.

3. Quoted by Quentin Anderson, *Making Americans: An Essay on Individualism and Money*, New York: Harcourt, Brace, 1992.

4. *Ibid.*

5. In addition to MacIntyre's *After Virtue*, see Peter Berger, 'On the Obsolescence of the Concept of Honor', in *Facing Up to Modernity*, New York: Basic Books, 1977; and C. S. Lewis, *The Abolition of Man*, Oxford: OUP, 1943.

6. See Philip Rieff, *The Triumph of the Therapeutic*, New York: 1966, and *Fellow Teachers*, New York, 1972, revised edition, Chicago: University of Chicago Press, 1991.

7. See Nikolai Zernov, *The Russian Religious Renaissance of the Twentieth Century*, London: Barton, Longman, and Todd, 1963, *passim.*

8. Quoted by John Updike, *Picked-Up Pieces*, Greenwich, Conn.: Fawcett, 1975, p. 15.

9. See, for example, Renée Winegarten, *Writers and Revolution*, New York: Franklin Watts, 1974, pp. 202–208.

10. For a fine, short, jargon-free essay on 'orthodox irony' as here conceived, see Hilaire Belloc, 'On Irony', reprinted in J. B. Morton (ed.), *Selected Essays of Hilaire Belloc*, London: Methuen, 1948, pp. 17–20.

11. Updike, *op. cit.*, p. 143.

12. See Zernov, *op. cit.*, pp. 285–298, and *passim.*

13. Dostoevsky, *The Devils*, 1871, English translation, London: 1953, 1971, p. 197; *cf.* p. 696.

14. Dostoevsky, *Notes from Underground*, 1864, English translation, New York: Dutton, 1960, p. 8; *cf.* S. L. Frank's 'The Ethics of Nihilism', 1909, in Zernov, *op. cit.*, pp. 115–116.

15. Dostoevsky, *The Devils*, *op. cit.*, p. 692.

16. Introduction to Dostoevsky, *The Notebooks for 'The Possessed'*, Chicago: University of Chicago Press, 1968, p. 1.

17. On Polanyi's Dostoevskian insights, see Thomas F. Torrance, *Theology in Reconciliation*, London: Geoffrey Chapman, 1975, pp. 275–277; and Torrance's *Belief in Science and the Christian Life: The Relevance of Michael Polanyi's Thought for Christian Faith and Life*, Edinburgh: Handsell, 1980.

18. Quoted by Max Hayward, Introduction to Alexander Gladkov, *Meetings with Pasternak: A Memoir*, New York: Harcourt, Brace, 1977, p. 29.

19. Valéry, quoted by E. J. Oliver in his Foreword to Christopher Dawson, *The Gods of Revolution*, New York: Funk and Wagnalls/Minerva, 1972, p. xiv; Dostoevsky, quoted by V. Borisov in *From Under the Rubble*, A. Solzhenitsyn, et. al., Boston: Little, Brown, 1975, p. 202.

20. *The Diary of a Writer*, translated by B. Brasol, London: Cassell, 1949, Vol. 1, p. 149.

21. *The Devils*, p. 126.

22. Quoted in Mihajlo Mihajlov, *Underground Notes*, Kansas City: Sheed, Andrews, and McMeel, 1976, pp. 62–63; *cf.*, A. Solzhenitsyn, *The Gulag Archipelago*, Vol. 2, 'The Ascent'; and Philip Rieff, 'The Newer Noises of War', *op. cit.*, p. 360: 'The *psychomachia* is no less permanent than the *kulturkampf* '.

Chapter 2

1. There is, of course, no golden age of virtue. For all its *douceur de la vie*, the French *Ancien Régime* was profligate and licentious. It produced Rousseau, in whom may be seen every modern vice, and suppressed the Jansenists. By contrast, the revolutionaries of 1789 were a good deal more concerned about virtue. Compare David to Fragonard, or Robespierre to Talleyrand, who symbolized the values of the *Ancien Régime* long after its passing. If one prefers the *Ancien Régime*, as I do, then one must prize not only virtue, but also such values as hierarchy, ritual, gentleness, and an aesthetic sensibility. That said, no one would confuse the *Ancien Régime* with the modern world.

2. See, for example, Jayne Levin, 'A Case of Rent, Bias and Religious Views; In California Landlords Deny Apartment to Unmarried Couple', *Washington Post,* July 15, 1994, p. F1; a similar case is currently being litigated in Massachusetts; see *AG* v. *Desilets*, 418 Mass. 316 (SJC 1994).

3. *Madsen* v. *Women's Health Clinic*, 114 S. Ct. 2516 (1994).

4. On 18th-century anti-Catholic laws see Sir William Blackstone, *IV Commentaries on the Law of England* 54–56 (15th edition, 1809). Though

no friend of Catholics, Blackstone looked forward to the repeal of such laws, and supported toleration so long as the Hanoverian dynasty and the established church were secure. *Ibid.*, 50–51; 56–57. For Blackstone on blasphemy, see *ibid.*, 59.

5. See Cass Sunstein, 'Legal Interference with Personal Preferences', *University of Chicago Legal Review*, 1129, 1986, p. 53.

6. See John H. DiIulio, 'Five Crime Bills—Better than (N)One', *The Wall Street Journal*, August 16, 1994, p. A12.

7. Boswell attributed the authorship of these lines to Johnson, to whom Goldsmith turned for help with the poem.

8. Under contingency fee arrangements, clients do not pay their lawyers for legal fees, but split any award with them. In addition, the losing party to an American suit does not have to pay expensive court costs, as he would in England or Canada. Add to this the readiness of courts to invent new torts, and of juries to grant fabulous awards for trivial wrongs, and one has the litigation explosion described by Walter Olsen. See Walter K. Olsen, *The Litigation Explosion*, Thomas Talley Books/Dutton, 1991.

9. *Ibid.*, pp. 152–153.

10. *Kirksey* v. *Kirksey*, 8 Ala. 131 (Sup. Ct., 1845).

11. See Adrian Furnham, 'Fortitude: The Modern Tendencies to Narcissism and Blaming Others', in Digby Anderson (ed), *The Loss of Virtue: Moral Confusion and Social Disorder in Britain and America*, National Review/Social Affairs Unit, 1992, p. 135.

12. *Victorian Railway Commissioners* v. *Coultas*, 13 App. Cast. 222 (183 PC).

13. See A. J. McClurg, 'It's a Wonderful Life: The Case for Hedonic Damages in Wrongful Death Cases', *Notre Dame Law Review*, 66, 1990, p. 57.

14. A generous jury also awarded her $3 million for the jackpot even though the official rule book specified that such contestants were not winners. See Olsen, *op. cit.*, note 8, pp. 170–171. For a further parade of horribles, see Christopher J. Sykes, *A Nation of Victims: The Decay of the American Character*, St. Martin's Press, 1992, pp. 124–134.

15. A computer search through Lexis law review files does not reveal any support for restrictions on claims for emotional distress. A similar search in Lexis case files is more likely to turn up decisions which commend a plaintiff's fortitude in litigating, or which question his fortitude in continuing to work after an injury without seeking professional help.

16. *I Commentaries*, Introduction, section 1, p. 34.

17. For a summary of public choice principles see Dennis C. Mueller, *Public Choice II*, Cambridge University Press, 1989, particularly pp. 247–268.

18. Grant Gilmore, *The Ages of American Law*, Vol. 3, Yale University Press, 1977.

19. *Hinz* v. *Berry*, [1970] 2 QB 40, 42.

20. Lord Denning, *The Closing Chapter*, Butterworths, 1983, pp. 18–19.

Chapter 3

1. J. Fitzjames Stephen, *Liberty, Equality, Fraternity*, Indianapolis: Liberty Fund, 1993, p. 53.

2. André Gide, *If It Die*, Penguin, 1951, p. 277.

3. It may also be objected that the idea of necrophilia being taken seriously is fantastic. As this book goes to press, an appeal is being lodged in the European Court of Human Rights for sado-masochism to be ruled acceptable—for consenting adults.

Chapter 5

1. Some public schools in the Los Angeles area have tried uniforms and have found an improvement in grades and a decrease in gang-related incidents.

2. It is obviously the narcissism of the '60's generation' adults that is at work here, for they are today's parents and teachers. The penchant to be the child's 'buddy' is a form of *self*-indulgence. Its value to the child is questionable.

3. In the same vein, one can only hope that we need not give any response to the notion that uniforms are inherently religious and that therefore their general use would illicitly mix church and state.

4. Children are quite able to establish their own signs of status even within a uniform system. In one case with which I am familiar, girls do so by wearing bits of jewellery in addition to the uniform. Yet these displays of status occur within a context set by adults. When children, on the other hand, decide the context, not only are certain elements of arbitrariness, injustice, and possibly cruelty more likely to be a factor in determining who is 'in' and who is not, but also the role of status itself is heightened.

5. It was common in the past, however, for immigrants to the U.S. to want their children to be Americans at school and then, perhaps, members of their ancestral culture at home. They understood that success in society can only come by some form of significant assimilation. In the welfare state, however, it may be that since everyone's success is guaranteed, assimilation is less important.

6. It is not repression itself that has value, but the fostering of right desire. For an Aristotelian, it is action based on desire that should ultimately be encouraged. Doing the good because one desires it is better than doing the good. One gets that sort of desire, however, by first habituating oneself to it.

Chapter 8

1. H. Schoeck, *Envy: A Theory of Social Behaviour*, London: Secker and Warburg, 1969, p. 57.

2. For an early comparative statement of the problem as far as America is concerned, see Robert King Merton, 'Social Structure and Anomie', in *Social Theory and Social Structure*, Glencoe, New York: Free Press, 1957.

3. As I was writing this chapter in my office in Reading, England, a fax arrived from a concerned lawyer in Wisconsin seeking my advice about the 'lawyer joke problem'.

4. For details see R. Brandon and C. Davies, *Wrongful Imprisonment: Mistaken Convictions and Their Consequences*, London: Allen and Unwin, 1973.

5. *Ibid.*

6. The details are to be found in *US News and World Report*, 1991.

Chapter 9

1. Aristotle, 'Posterior Analytics', in R. M. Hutchins (ed.), *Great Books of the Western World*, Chicago: Encyclopedia Britannica, Vol. 8, 1952, p. 128.

2. Aristotle, 'Physics', in R. M. Hutchins, *ibid.*, pp. 276, 277.

3. Francis Bacon, 'Advancement of Learning', in R. M. Hutchins, *ibid.*, Vol. 30, p. 45.

4. *Ibid.*, p. 44.

5. See J. F. Rychlak, 'Technical Problems with Teleological Explanation in Psychopathology: Sigmund Freud as a Case in Point', in M. Spitzer and B. A. Maher (eds.), *Philosophy and Psychopathology*, New York: Springer-Verlag, 1990, pp. 102–117.

6. S. Freud, 'The Psychotherapy of Everyday Life', 1901, republished in J. Strachey (ed.), *The Standard Edition of the Complete Psychological Works of Sigmund Freud*, Vol. 8, London: Hogarth, 1960, pp. 6–7.

7. S. Freud 'Jokes and Their Relation to the Unconscious', 1905, republished in Strachey, *op. cit.*, p. 175.

8. S. Freud, 'The Case of a Successful Treatment by Hypnotism', 1892, republished in Strachey, *op. cit.*, Vol. 1, 1966, pp. 115–128.

9. S. Freud, 'Obsessive Actions and Religious Practices', 1907, republished in Strachey, *op. cit.*, Vol. 9, 1959, pp. 115–127.

10. For example, see S. Freud, 'The Psychoanalytic View of Psychogenic Disturbance of Vision', 1910, republished in Strachey, *op. cit.*, Vol. 11, 1957, p. 213.

11. For example, see S. Freud, 'Psychoanalytic Notes on an Autobiographical Account of a Case of Paranoia (The Case of Schreber)', 1911, republished in Strachey, *op. cit.*, Vol. 12, 1958, pp. 66–68.

12. S. Freud, 'Psychoanalysis and Telepathy', 1921, republished in Strachey, *op. cit.*, Vol. 18, 1955, pp. 173–193.

13. *Ibid.*, p. 185.

14. S. Freud, 'The Future Prospects of Psychoanalytic Therapy', 1910, republished in Strachey, *op. cit.*, Vol. 11, 1957, p. 150.

15. J. B. Watson, *Behaviorism*, New York: W. W. Norton & Co., 1924, p. 216; italics in original.

16. W. L. Reese, *Dictionary of Philosophy and Religion: Eastern and Western Thought*, Atlantic Highlands, N.J.: Humanities Press, 1980, p. 345; D. D. Runes, *Dictionary of Philosophy*, New York: Philosophical Library, 1960, p. 194.

17. B. F. Skinner, *Verbal Behavior*, New York: Appleton-Century-Crofts, 1957, p. 460.

18. H. Gardner, *The Mind's New Science: A History of the Cognitive Revolution*, New York: Basic Books, 1985.

19. J. F. Rychlak, *Artificial Intelligence and Human Reason: A Teleological Critique*, New York: Columbia University Press, 1991, pp. 86–88.

20. For example, see R. C. Schank & R. P. Abelson, *Scripts, Plans, Goals and Understanding*, Hillsdale, N.J.: Erlbaum, 1977, p. 69.

21. For example, see J. F. Rychlak, *Logical Learning Theory: A Human Teleology and its Empirical Support*, Lincoln, Neb.: University of Nebraska Press, 1994.

22. Watson, *op. cit.*, p. 216.

23. Rychlak, 1991, *op. cit.*

Chapter 10

1. Martin Jacques, 'The Erosion of the Establishment', *The Sunday Times*, January 16, 1994, pp. 5–9.

2. This is despite the fact that there is a debate over the relative importance of armed forces compared with other instruments of policy for a state seeking to defend its interests in today's new security climate.

3. S. Glover, 'Why Tories Must Break with the Past', *Evening Standard*, October 27, 1993, p. 9, col. 2.

4. See M. Jacques, 'The Culture Essay', *Sunday Times*, June 12, 1994, pp. 8–10; M. Lyn, 'Redundancies Focus on the White-collar Worker', *Sunday Times Business*, March 20, 1994, p. 5.

5. K. Marx, *Manifesto of the Communist Party*, reprinted in L. S. Feuer (ed.), *Marx and Engels, Basic Writings on Politics and Philosophy*, Collins, Fontana, 1969, pp. 51–52.

6. See C. Dandeker, 'A Farewell to Arms? The Military and the Nation

State in a Changing World', in J. Burk (ed.), *The Military in New Times: Adapting Armed Forces to a Turbulent World*, Westview, 1994, pp. 117–140; C. Dandeker, 'New Times for the Military: Some Sociological Remarks on the Changing Role and Structure of the Armed Forces of the Advanced Societies', *British Journal of Sociology*, December 1994.

7. P. Dicken, *Global Shift, Industrial Change in a Turbulent World*, Harper and Row, 1986; D. Held, 'Farewell the Nation-State?', *Marxism Today*, December 12–17, 1988; A. Giddens, *The Consequences of Modernity*, Polity, 1992; P. Kennedy, *Preparing for the Twenty First Century*, Random House, 1993, pp. 47–64.

8. A. Mesny, 'Globalisation, Communication et Guerre du Golfe', in M. Audet and Bouchikhi, *Structuration du social et Modernité avancée*, University of Laval Press, 1993, pp. 223–30.

9. Dicken, *op. cit.*, pp. 293–312.

10. Kennedy, *op. cit.*, pp. 122–34; P. Alter, *Nationalism*, Edward Arnold, pp. 119–24.

11. Kennedy, *ibid.*; M. Weller, 'Nationalism; Breaking Up is Hard to Do', *New Statesman and Society*, August 23, 1991, pp. 18–19.

12. C. Moskos and J. Burk, 'A Post-Modern Military', in J. Burk, *op. cit.*, pp. 141–162.

13. M. Jacques, 'The Erosion . . . ', *op. cit.*, p. 7.

14. E. Durkheim, *The Division of Labour in Society*, Free Press/Macmillan, 1968, p. 227.

15. *Ibid.*, p. 228.

16. C. Dandeker, 'Service and National Service: the Obligations of Citizenship', in D. Anderson (ed.), *The Loss of Virtue: Moral Confusion and Social Disorder In Britain and America*, National Review/Social Affairs Unit, 1992, pp. 83–96.

17. The key work is C. Moskos and F. R. Wood, *The Military: More than Just a Job?*, Pergamon Brassey's, 1988.

18. C. Moskos, *Soldiers and Sociology*, U.S. Army Research Institute for the Behavioral and Social Sciences, 1988, p. 59.

19. *Ibid.*, p. 60.

20. See F. R. Wood, 'At the Cutting Edge of Institutional and Occupational Trends: The U.S. Air Force Officer Corps', in Moskos and Wood, *op. cit.*, p. 30.

21. On some of these issues see C. Dandeker and G. Harries Jenkins, 'The Employment of Homosexuals in Armed Forces: Operational, Social and Political Problems—A View from the United Kingdom', in S. Stanley and W. Scott (eds.), *Sexual Orientation and Military Service*, De Gruyter, 1994.

22. Major M. J. Perry, 'A Military Federation for Britain's Armed Forces', *British Army Review*, No. 107, August 1994.

23. D. R. Segal, 'Measuring the Institution/Occupation Hypothesis', *Armed Forces and Society*, Vol. 12, No. 3, 1986, pp. 351–376.

24. I owe this point to Anthony Giddens. Similar views were expressed by Max Weber in his essay 'Science as a Vocation', in H. Gerth and C. Wright Mills, *From Max Weber: Essays in Sociology*, Routledge, 1970, pp. 129–156.

25. This point is developed by James Burk in his introduction to J. Burk, *op. cit.*, pp. 12, 20–22.

Chapter 11

1. *Characteristics*, Miscellany IV, Indianapolis: Bobbs-Merrill, 1964, Chapter 2, p. 295.

2. Reports on the recent work of David Selbourne, *The Principle of Duty*,

suggest the correctness of this approach, even if he errs in blaming the American Revolution for the decline.

3. S. C. Brubaker, 'Can Liberals Punish?', *APSR*, 82.3, 1988, pp. 821–835.

4. Richard C. Morais, 'ME! Me! Me!', a review of Selbourne's *The Principle of Duty*, *Forbes*, September 12, 1994, p. 90.

5. Brubaker, *op. cit.*, p. 825.

Chapter 12

1. Augustine, *De Civitate Dei*, 15.22.

2. Augustine, *De Spiritu et Littera*, 63.

3. G. Guiver, *Faith in Momentum*, London: SPCK, 1990, p. 28.

4. Augustine, *Epistolae*, 185 ('De Correctione Donatistarum').

5. See, J. Delumeau, *Le Péché et la peur. Le culpabilisation en Occident XIIIe-XVIIIe Siècles*, Paris: Payard, 1983; and Ralph Gibson, *A Social History of French Catholicism, 1789–1914*, London: Routledge, 1989.

6. Martin Luther, 'Secular Authority: To What Extent It Should Be Obeyed', in *Works of Martin Luther*, Vol. 3, Philadelphia: A. J. Holman Co. and the Castle Press, 1930, p. 236.

Chapter 13

1. Alexander Hamilton, John Jay, and James Madison, Chapter 1 in George W. Carey and James McClellan (eds.), *The Federalist*, Kendall/Hunt, 1990, p. 5.

2. For a particularly lucid defence of the city may I recommend the funeral oration of Pericles set forth in Book II of Thucydides' *The History of the Peloponnesian War*.

3. I should note at this point that of all social scientists, it seems that social psychologists have made the most progress in the study of the effects of the urban setting on the psyche of man. For those seeking a good introduction to the cognitive and non-cognitive influences of urban life, I suggest an examination of the work of Claude Fischer, *The Urban Experience.*

4. Thomas Hobbes, *Leviathan,* Cambridge, 1992, Part I, Chapter XI, p. 69.

5. For a particularly lucid and cogent account of the meaning and limits of the ancient city, may I suggest Fustel de Coulanges, *The Ancient City*, Johns Hopkins University Press, 1980.

6. See, for example, Robert Lynch, *The Image of the City*, MIT Press, 1960.

7. For an insisghtful understanding of modern-day positivism and its effects upon architecture, see Alberto Perez-Gomez, *Architecture and the Crisis of Modern Science*, MIT Press, 1983.